Teacher: "And what does your daddy do?"

Alex, aged 6: "He spits out wine..."

To Alex, the Insomniac Wanderer, who hasn't had a book dedicated to him until now.

About the author

Wine Consultant, Author and Speaker Simon Woods has won awards for his writing, his website and his can-can dancing. While he spits out most of the thousands of wines he tastes each year, he does confess to swallowing a few of them.

When he's not visiting vineyards, tasting with importers and retailers, or hosting one of the dozens of wine events he conducts each year, he can be found at home with his family in Saddleworth in the north of England.

You can sign up for his weekly newsletter at simonwoods.com, or catch his videos on his YouTube channel MrWoodswine.

www.simonwoods.com
@woodswine
facebook.com/simonwoodswine

Other books by Simon Woods
I Don't Know Much About Wine But I Know What I Like
The World's Shortest Wine Book

101 Wine FAQs

The answers to
the questions
that people ask
about wine

Simon Woods

101 Wine FAQs

by Simon Woods

First edition published in 2017 by Simon Woods, 37 Wool Road, Dobcross, Oldham OL3 5NS, UK

ISBN-13: 978-0-9930006-2-1

ISBN-10: 0-9930006-2-2

Contents

"I don't know if this is a stupid question but…"

I conduct dozens of wine tastings each year, and people say I'm very good at them. But I haven't always been…

No one actually fell asleep at any of my early attempts to pass on my knowledge about wine, but I certainly induced more than a few yawns. It wasn't a shortage of information that was the problem. In fact it was the opposite. I had so much to tell people and I did my darnedest to pack as much as possible into the time available.

However, I soon discovered that the specialised language of wine isn't universally spoken. I'm so thankful to those people who stuck their hands up and said, "I don't know if this is a stupid question but what did you mean when you said…"

The first few times, it stopped me in my tracks. Didn't everyone know what a grape variety was? Or what "cuvée" meant? Or that keeping bottles upright by the kitchen stove was a bad idea?

But then it dawned on me. I might have had lots of information to present, but it wasn't necessarily what people – normal people, not those who spend a lot of time spitting into buckets – wanted to know. I was answering questions that they were not asking.

So from then onwards, I've made a point of encouraging my audiences to ask questions. Occasionally some of them ARE a bit stupid: "In the 1980s, I used to buy a wine when I was on holiday in Spain that had a brown label – what would it have been?" Or: "Is wine in big bottles stronger than wine in smaller ones?"

But most of the time, the questions come from a desire to know just a little more. So over the past 20 years, I've been compiling a list of those questions, and this book is my attempt to answer 101 of the most popular, interesting and useful ones that have cropped up.

With some questions, this is straightforward. With others, the question may be simple, but the answer could very well run to a doctoral thesis. So if there are some answers here where you think I've only skimmed the surface, get in touch on Twitter or Facebook and I'll see if I can point you in the direction of more information.

Contact me too if there are questions that you think I've missed out. If there are enough of them, I may just have to write a sequel...

Simon Woods
August 2017

*I have a
question
about...*

The Origins
of Wine

1-6

1 | when was wine first made?

2 | which country makes the most wine?

3 | which country drinks the most wine?

4 | what are the 10 best-selling wines in the world?

5 | what's your favourite wine?

6 | what is "fine" wine?

1| when was wine first made?

The first wine would have made itself, with air-borne yeasts initiating fermentation of the juice that oozed from a bucketful of grapes in the warm sun. The oldest winery that has so far been unearthed is in southern Armenia and dates back to around 4100 BC. But there's evidence from Georgia of wine being produced two thousand years before that, in the form of residues on the insides of ancient clay storage jars.

2| which country makes the most wine?

The figures below are estimates for 2016 production in '000s of hectolitres from the International Organisation of Vine and Wine (OIV). Italy and France usually fight it out for top slot, but watch out for China in coming years – only Spain has a larger area of vineyards, even if most of the Chinese production is for eating grapes rather than wine.

Italy	50,900
France	43,500
Spain	39,300
United States	23,900
Australia	13,000
China	11,400
South Africa	10,500
Chile	10,100
Argentina	9,400
World total	**267,000**

3 | which country drinks the most wine?

Do you mean per person, or in total? Might as well give you the latest stats at the time of writing.

Per person	In total
1. Italy	1. USA
2. France	2. France
3. Switzerland	3. Italy
4. Portugal	4. Germany
5. Austria	5. China + Hong Kong
6. Greece	6. United Kingdom
7. Denmark	7. Argentina
8. Germany	8. Russia
9. Argentina	9. Spain
10. Hungary	10. Australia

4 | what are the 10 best-selling wines in the world?

I've struggled to find data on specific wines, how about I give you the 10 biggest selling brands (as of 2015)?

1. Barefoot (USA)	6. Yellow Tail (Australia)
2. Gallo (USA)	7. Hardys (Australia)
3. Concha y Toro (Chile)	8. Lindeman's (Australia)
4. Robert Mondavi (USA)	9. Beringer (USA)
5. Sutter Home (USA)	10. Jacob's Creek (Australia)

5 | what's your favourite wine?

If I had £1 for every time I've been asked this question...
Now, I usually turn it back on the questioner and ask them
things like what's their favourite song, or their favourite
food, or their favourite item of clothing. All things like this
depend on the circumstances – where you are, whom
you're with, what sort of mood you're in, and so on. So
when it comes to wine, I want a whole smorgasbord,
wardrobe, playlist of the stuff – confining me to just one
type would be to miss out on so much of the pleasure of
the subject.

So that's my diplomatic answer. The true answer is really
good red Burgundy.

6 | what is "fine" wine?

I've seen many people try to answer this question, only to
end up sounding like a pompous git, with words like
"typicity" and "complexity" being bandied about. Others
resort to financial terms, and say that fine wine is
something for which there is an excess of demand over
supply, resulting in a "secondary market" in which prices
could possibly rise.

At a time such as this, maybe the best course of action is
to refer to the ever-entertaining Urban Dictionary: "Fine
wine is wine that is finer than most..." Very true. I'll leave
other people to discuss how to define "finer" and "most"
and move on. Although maybe I'd add in that for me, a

fine wine is one that I don't get bored of. On that criterion, an awful lot of expensive wines would miss the cut, while several rather cheaper ones would be included.

A common coda to the question is, "What is the [INSERT SUPERLATIVE] wine in the world?" Three versions usually crop up – sometimes, it's the best wine in the world, sometimes the rarest, sometimes the most expensive. Might as well go through them one by one...

1) The best wine. Sorry, wine isn't a "first past the post" type of subject. What's the best music in the world, or the best painting?

2) The rarest wine. Not sure why people want to know this. Just because something is made in tiny amounts doesn't mean it's any good. If you want to know the rarest that's currently available from any winery, Seppeltsfield in the Barossa Valley in Australia probably takes the crown. At the time of writing (summer 2017), there are less than ten 100ml bottles of the 1880 (yes, 1880) Para Tawny available – price AUS$2,450 each.

3) The most expensive wine. Of current releases, Romanée Conti from Domaine de la Romanée Conti in Burgundy comes out top – the 2012 will set you back around £10,000 for a bottle. Yes, a bottle. Of older wines, you're looking at the three bottles of 1869 Château Lafite sold at auction in Hong Kong in 2010 – for US$230,000 each...

I have a question about...

How Wine Is Made

7-18

7 | how is wine made?

It begins with grapes. Let's talk red wine first. Peel most red grapes – Pinot Noir, Malbec, Shiraz, whatever – and eventually you'll have a pile of dark skin and a pale piece of fruit. The skin is home to nearly all the grape's colour and tannin and much of the flavour. Meanwhile our naked grape is home to virtually all the sugar, water and acidity.

Rather than peel grapes, winemakers usually give them a squeeze – sometimes light, sometimes heavy – to split their skins and release the grape juice. Then it's time for fermentation, the conversion of sugar into alcohol under the influence of yeast. That sugar is hopefully provided by the grapes themselves, although sometimes a little is added (more about that later on in this section). As for the yeast, there is some naturally present on the grapes and in the atmosphere, but while some producers rely on this, others are more cautious and add some of their own.

How long the fermentation takes depends on factors such as the sugar in the grapes and the temperature in the fermenting vessel. But all the while, those grape skins are macerating in the mixture. The longer they stay there, and the more the mixture is stirred, the more colour, flavour and tannin end up in the wine. It's like making tea – longer brew = stronger brew. Fermentation complete, the wine is drained off the skins, which are sometimes given an extra squeeze, like squeezing the last drops out of a teabag.

And that's your basic red. It might be bottled almost immediately, once any grungy bits have been removed, it might be blended with other batches, or it might go into barrels for further aging (see the next chapter).

White wines differ in that the grapeskins are usually discarded when the grapes are crushed, although some producers allow an hour or so of "skin contact" to add a little character. And there's now a vogue for "orange wines", in which the white grapes are treated in the same way as red, with macerations lasting weeks, even months. The results are fascinating and unusual: wines that are deep gold in colour with a fair whack of tannin. But they're not for everyone...

8 | why are wines aged in oak?

Once upon a time, various types of wood were used for vessels both for the storage and transport of not just wine but many other products. Oak rose to the top as the winemakers' preferred option for a number of reasons. It was strong, it was available, it wasn't too porous, it could be bent into shape fairly easily and – unlike pine, for example – it didn't mar the flavour of the wines.

In fact, as winemaking developed, producers began to realise that oak barrels could have a positive effect on their wines. The obvious one is flavour. The barrel staves are usually bent into shape by holding them close to a fire, and this heat not only temporarily softens the wood, making it more flexible, but also "toasts" some of the compounds in the oak. This leads to flavours such as coconut, vanilla, cloves and – yes – fresh toast which are then transferred to the wine stored in the finished barrel. Most of these flavours come out the first time the barrels are used, less the second time, even less the third time until by around the fourth time, there's little flavour left. So why don't wineries just renew their barrels each year?

Cost is a major issue. A new barrique – a typical size, holding around 225 litres/300 bottles – costs hundreds, even thousands of pounds. But another factor is that not all producers want that intensity of oak flavour, as it can overwhelm the more delicate characters in their wines. Instead, they'll use some new barrels, some that are one year old, some two years old and so on.

In which case, you say, why use older barrels at all? Why not just age some of the wine in new oak and the rest of the blend in a large tank? It's because a barrel doesn't just give flavour to a wine, it also helps round out its rougher edges. The wine in effect "breathes" through the pores in the oak, becoming softer and mellower in the process. Some wines are in oak for just a few months, others for a couple of years and some – certain Madeiras and tawny ports for example – are kept in barrels for decades.

A final word about oak. Not all oak is equal. There are different species of oak, and even when you have the same species, they grow at different rates depending on where the trees are planted. The two main types you'll see mentioned are French oak and American oak. American oak is cheaper, and – to generalise vastly – gives more intense but less subtle flavours to a wine than French.

9 | what is organic wine? and biodynamic?

Wine is no different from any other agricultural product in that when the growing season is less than ideal, the growers often resort to less natural means to make up for nature's deficiencies. For a run-down of what apart from grapes can make its way into wine, see Chapter 17. Rely too much on more than a few of these and you end up with a wine so dosed up with chemicals and other additives that it's as much a product of the lab as the vineyard. It's stable but sterile. At the other extreme, you have wines with zero additives that are as close to nature as they can be – and sometimes that means being a bit too close for comfort and pleasure.

Somewhere between these polar opposites, a variety of organisations have set boundaries as to what constitutes an organic wine. While the precise rules vary depending on which organisation made them, in general you can say that a wine certified as organic is made with reduced chemical interference in both vineyard and winery.

However, while it may be healthier, both for people and for the environment, that doesn't mean that organic wine is better than non-organic: that's far more dependent on the skill of the producer. In addition, there are many producers who prefer not to seek out organic certification yet whose wines are made with very little jiggery-pokery.

Biodynamic wine is often thought of as a subset of organic, but that's not quite the case. Biodynamics includes conducting various agricultural operations – pruning, picking etc. – in accordance with phases of the moon, and using certain preparations in tiny quantities to aid plant growth. Most practitioners also stick to organic principles, but there's more of a focus on working with the rhythms of nature. Whatever they are.

As for natural wine, that's the second of those polar opposites I mentioned above. Wine as nature intended, wine stripped bare. And as with people stripped bare, sometimes it's a beautiful thing to behold, and sometimes, you wish there was something there to mask the more unsightly aspects...

10 | how is rosé wine made?

There are two main ways. Firstly, you can blend red and white wines. Do you see anything problematic with that? Does that sounds offensive to you? Is that a major wine crime? Nay, nay and thrice nay is my answer, but for some reason, producers in certain parts of Europe disapprove of this way of making rosé and would like to ban it.

For method two, let's skip back to that bit about making tea in Chapter 7. Do you have any friends who are what I call 10-second-teabag people, as in they won't drink any cuppa that's been brewed for longer? The result is pale and – to me at least – not all that interesting, but that's how they like it. Rosé can be made in a very similar way, with the skins macerating in the grape juice for just a few hours until the desired colour is achieved.

11 | how is sparkling wine made?

In the process of fermentation, the sugar in grape juice is transformed into alcohol and carbon dioxide. So the simplest way of making a sparkling wine is to bottle it part-way through fermentation while there's still some unfermented sugar and allow the process to finish in the bottle. These so-called Pet-Nat wines (short for pétillant naturel or natural sparkling) have enjoyed a surge in popularity in recent times. Yes, they still contain some yeasty deposits (AKA lees), but for many fans, this only adds to their charm.

But most other sparkling wines are made by taking a still wine and then adding bubbles. At its most basic, this can be done by injecting carbon dioxide in what amounts to an industrial-size Sodastream. And if you've ever used a Sodastream, you know that drinks made in this way can be OK to begin with but soon lose their fizz. So better sparklers make use of the principle that fermentation produces both alcohol and carbon dioxide. Their producers make a regular wine and then add "liqueur de tirage" – basically some sugar and yeast dissolved in a little wine. They then put all the mixture in a sealed container and allow another fermentation to take place.

They can do this in two ways. The tank or Charmat method sees this additional fermentation (prise de mousse for techies) take place in a large pressurised container. The process takes a few weeks and the resulting wine can be bottled almost immediately. Prosecco is made this way. Or they can do it the way they do in Champagne and let the secondary fermentation take place in a wine bottle. Which makes removing the lees (which the Pet-Nat brigade don't object to, but a lot of people do) more complicated...

If the wine's in a tank, the lees will settle at the bottom of the tank, and the clear wine can then be siphoned off. If it's in a bottle however, each individual bottle needs to be jiggled until it's upside down and the lees are nestling on top of the cork (actually it's usually a beer-bottle-like crown cap). Once upon a time, this jiggling was done by wobbly-handed men, but today, there are special machines that do the task. Eventually, the bottles are plunged into an icy bath, the lees solidify into a grungy ice-cube, the cap is whipped off, and the yeasty plug removed.

For both methods, the longer you leave the wine on the lees, the more those carbon dioxide bubbles will dissolve into the wine, the longer they'll keep popping up from the bottom of your glass when the wine is eventually opened, and the smaller and finer those bubbles will be. Also, the lees contribute a nutty/biscuity richness, adding an extra layer of character to the wine.

Job done? Not quite. Prior to bottling in the Charmat method, or recorking in the Champagne method, the producer can add a small amount of a sugar-rich liquid called dosage. Think of this as correcting the seasoning of a dish just prior to serving – in this instance, the dosage is there to counter any tartness in the wine. Just as with salt in cooking, different people have different definitions of what is the correct dosage to produce the right balance. Also, the longer the aging on the lees, the rounder the wine will be, so the dosage can be reduced accordingly. Then it's on with the cork, complete with wire cage to stop it flying off into orbit when it shouldn't do, and your wine is finally ready. Simple. Ish...

12 | how is sweet wine made?

It is possible to make sweet wines simply by adding sugar or grape juice to a wine, but it seldom makes anything exciting. The good ones fall into five types – shrivelled, rotten, frozen, fortified and halted. Shrivelled and rotten wines first, as they have much in common. The longer you leave grapes to ripen, the more sugar (and less acidity) they'll have. Leave them long enough and – providing they've not been snaffled by birds, boars and other sugar-seeking beasts – one of two things will happen.

If conditions are reasonably dry, the grapes will start to shrivel, leaving them with less juice, but the same amount of sugar. You can leave them to shrivel naturally on the vine in the autumn sunshine, or you can give them a helping hand by picking them and allowing them to dry on straw mats – you may see some wines labelled straw wine or, in French, vin de paille – or in special drying rooms.

If there's some humidity, the grapes will start to rot. This doesn't sound very promising, and in many cases, it isn't. But if the humidity of the morning gives way to a warm dry afternoon, allowing the grapes to dry out, what is known as noble rot (AKA Botrytis Cinerea) can develop. Botrytis consumes sugar but it also dehydrates the grape, resulting (again) in juice with a greater sugar level. In addition, it produces various compounds including glycerol that add to the flavour and mouthfeel of the wine. The grapes look dreadful, but the rich toasty apricot and honey flavours in the resulting wines make picking them worthwhile. And since botrytis doesn't strike a vineyard all in one go, some producers will send their pickers through the vineyards several times over the course of a few weeks to harvest only the nobly-rotten grapes.

What happens when these sugar-rich grapes get to the winery is partly dictated by the winemaker and partly by the grapes themselves. If they're really sweet, then the yeast will get part of the way through turning that sugar to alcohol and then just give up, leaving lots of unfermented sweetness – residual sugar (RS) in winespeak. The extreme is the rare Tokaji Eszencia from Hungary, where in some years, the grape juice is around 90% sugar. Even after several years of fermentation, the alcohol level struggles to get much above 4%. If they're not quite that sweet, then the winemakers could in theory let the fermentations run their course and produce regular dry wines with a higher level of alcohol. However, many prefer to stop the fermentation before it's finished, leaving (again) residual sugar in the wine.

Thirdly, frozen. Icewine/Eiswein, a speciality of Germany, Austria and Canada, is made by allowing healthy grapes to linger on the vines well into winter, and harvesting only when they have frozen. The grapes are crushed, allowing chilly but still liquid nectar to ooze out while the ice stays in the press. The result is massively sweet and concentrated, and quite different from botrytis-affected sweet wine – I think of it being more intense but simpler.

The fourth type is fortified. Not all fortified wines are sweet – most sherry is dry for example. The sweeter styles are made by adding a neutral brandy at some stage in the fermentation. The earlier the spirit is added, the more unfermented sugar there'll be in the wine, and so the sweeter the wine will be. Port from Portugal is the most famous example, but there are examples in many other parts of the world. Occasionally spirit is added before fermentation has kicked in, in which case the wine is called a vin de liqueur – Pineau des Charentes from the Cognac region is the most famous.

Finally, halted. The grape juice may have the potential to make a wine at 13% alcohol, but the winemaker can stop the fermentation while there's still some unfermented sugar. It's a practice favoured in many cooler parts of the world where the juice has very high acidity. If the wine had been fermented to total dryness, that acidity would poke out sore-thumb-style. With lower alcohol and more sweetness, the wine is better balanced, as fans of Mosel Riesling Kabinett will very happily testify.

13 | what is fortified wine?

As I mentioned above, it's a regular wine to which neutral brandy spirit has been added. The first versions were made several centuries ago, when it was found that this helped preserve and stabilise wines that were being transported long distances, often by sea. Fortification may have started as a cautionary measure, but it wasn't long before wines such as sherry, port and Madeira developed an enthusiastic following in their own right.

Those three styles remain at the top of the fortified wine tree, but it's a mistake to think of them as similar wines. Sherry is perhaps the most misunderstood of the trio. In the UK, it's often seen as a rather fusty drink, and its image has been tarnished by numerous dubious sweet concoctions that in the past bore the name "Sherry". But the real stuff comes only from a small part of southern Spain, and ranges from pale and bone dry to deep and treacly in both colour and taste.

Fino and Manzanilla are the lightest, crispest styles, with alcohol levels typically around 15%. Treat them as you would a dry white wine – serve them chilled, and don't let the bottle hang around once opened. Their fresh, almost salty bite makes them perfect for tapas – or Pringles... Oloroso is a richer, darker wine, higher in alcohol (~19%) and with more of a nutty dried fruit character, while Amontillado sits between the two in style. Both are dry wines – drink them with savoury foods rather than puddings. Sweeter styles such as Cream Sherries are made by adding grape juice to dry wines. Sweetest of the lot is Pedro Ximénez, made from grapes that have been left in the sun to dry. Rich and raisinny, it's brilliant with good vanilla ice cream – drink some, pour some over the top.

Port comes from the Douro Valley in northern Portugal, with the name coming from the city of Oporto from which the wines have traditionally been shipped. While port exists in pink and white versions, it's the red wines that dominate production. Ports very roughly split into two camps – ruby and tawny. Both start in a similar way, with a wine being partially fermented and then spirit being added while there's still some unfermented sugar left in the mix.

Tawny ports spend several years aging in barrel, during which time they change from deep purple to a shade of brown in colour, losing some of their youthful freshness but acquiring more complex dried fruit and nut flavours. As they've done all their maturing in barrel, they're ready to drink on release. Ruby ports are bottled at an earlier stage, while there's more of the fresh fruit and spirity kick. Vintage port is the summit of the ruby port ladder, and thanks to its richness and structure, it can take 20 years or more to reach its peak. Late-bottled-vintage (LBV) offers something close to the vintage port experience, but is a fraction of the price and can be drunk at a far earlier stage.

Portugal's other fortified wine of note is Madeira. Quite different in flavour from port, it comes from a group of islands off the coast of North Africa, and it owes its style to its remote position. It was discovered around the 17th century that barrels of the wine that had undergone lengthy sea voyages to hot climes acquired a particular flavour that proved popular with many customers. The producers then began to duplicate the effect of this maturation by storing the barrels at their wineries in special rooms called estufas, in which they could "cook" under the rafters.

Today some producers continue to use a similar method to make Madeira, although others use large stainless steel tanks with heating pipes running through them to raise the temperature of the wines. The top wines are classified according to the grape from which they're made. In ascending order of sweetness, these are Sercial, Verdelho, Bual and Malmsey. The best combine intensity of nutty fig and raisin flavours with a tangy freshness. They're among the most long-lasting wines in the world, with bottles over 100 years old still tasting fresh and lively.

Other classic fortified wines made around the world include Marsala from Sicily, Banyuls and Maury from southern France, and Muscat and Topaque (formerly Tokay) from Rutherglen in Australia. All deserve a wider audience, especially at chillier times of the year.

14 | are wines made from one grape variety better than blends?

Are solo singers better than bands? Are dishes with just a handful of ingredients better than ones with several? Are magazines that cover just one topic better than those that cover many subjects? Some are, some aren't. So Riesling and Nebbiolo for example are at their best unblended, while Cabernet Sauvignon and Touriga Nacional are (for me) at their best with another grape or two in attendance.

15 | this wine is 8% alcohol, yet this one is 15% – why?

The principal source of alcohol in wines is the natural sugar in the grapes. During the process of fermentation, this sugar is converted by the action of yeast into alcohol and carbon dioxide – the higher the sugar level in the grapes, the higher the potential alcohol in the ultimate wine.

I'll come back to the "potential" bit in a moment. First, let's look at the three main reasons why those grapes might be higher in sugar. Firstly, that they come from a warmer place (Chapter 40 is all about how climate affects wine). Secondly, they were harvested later. During the growing season, the sugar in the grapes rises, while their acidity falls: just try a grape a couple of months before it's fully ripe, and the tartness will be almost unbearable.

Thirdly, yield, which is the quantity of fruit the vineyard produces and is measured either per vine or per hectare.

In general, the higher the yield, the more dilute the wine will be in both flavour and sugar. Think of it like a measure of cordial: do you use it for a small but intensely flavoured drink or something larger but weaker?

(There's also a fourth reason – evaporation. Pick your grapes on a very hot day, then take a while delivering them to the winery, and it's not uncommon for them to lose moisture, resulting in a rise in sugar levels. Sometimes the wineries do this in a more controlled fashion, letting their grapes dry over the course of several weeks in purpose-built facilities. Italy's Vin Santo and Amarone are probably the most famous examples.)

So the potential alcohol of a wine due solely to the grapes is dependent partly on nature, partly on nurture. However, the ACTUAL alcohol level of the wine could be either lower or higher.

It could be lower for a few reasons. The simplest one is what could be described as "post-fermentation irrigation", better known as dilution. Hey, people add water to their scotch, what's the problem with adding some to a wine? It's often done in warmer parts of the world, but seldom talked about.

Yeast also has an effect. Some yeasts are more efficient than others and produce a little more alcohol for every unit of sugar. Others are a bit wimpy and give up the ghost before all the sugar has been converted to alcohol, leaving the wine with some residual sugar (more about RS in the wine and calories section, Chapter 93).

But as you'll remember from Chapter 12, the winemaker might want to leave some RS in the wine, in which case they'll stop the fermentation, either through filtering out the yeast or by adding sulphur dioxide which stops it working. The result either way is a wine lower in alcohol than it could have been.

There are also special machines that use processes such as distillation or osmosis to adjust the level of alcohol, usually downwards, but sometimes, in cooler climates, upwards as well. A more common method of increasing alcohol in the chillier parts of Europe has been to add sugar (usually cane sugar, but sometimes beet sugar or corn syrup) during fermentation, a process known as chaptalisation.

Another substance that can be added to boost the alcohol level is...more alcohol! Fortified wines (see Chapter 13) have brandy or other spirits added at some point in their production to boost their strength. A typical port for example will be 20% grape brandy.

And finally, there can be an alteration in the alcohol level of a wine over the months and years that it is stored in barrel. In dry conditions, the alcohol will rise over time; in very humid conditions, it will fall.

16 | what gives a full-bodied wine its body?

It comes from a variety of sources.
1) Yield. Ask your vineyard for lots of fruit, and it will oblige, but the flavours will be dilute. Ask it for less and you'll get smaller amounts of fuller-bodied wine.

2) Make-up of grapes. Some grapes just have a greater concentration of polyphenols (the compounds responsible for flavour, colour, tannin etc.) than others.

3) Extraction. In other words, how much you squeeze the grapes to release those polyphenols. Higher extraction leads to darker, fleshier, more tannic wines.

4) Alcohol. The higher, the fuller.

5) Sugar. Ditto: a hint of residual sugar fattens up many supposedly dry whites and reds.

6) Alcoholic Fermentation. Some producers like to use certain strains of yeast that give wines with a richer mouthfeel.

7) Malolactic Fermentation. In which apple-y malic acid is converted to creamier lactic acid. Virtually all reds go through it, but it can also be used to soften and fatten white wines.

8) Oak. Fermenting and aging wines in barrel or with other oak products (see the next chapter) makes for richer, rounder wines.

9) Lees Aging. Keeping the wine in tank or barrel on the dead yeast cells after fermentation adds a biscuity depth.

But it's important to remember two things. Firstly that fuller body doesn't necessarily equate to better wine, just louder wine. There has been a welcome reaction against the bodybuilder style of wines that wooed certain critics throughout the 1990s in favour of gentler, more-user-friendly styles. Secondly, just because a wine has plenty of one or more of the substances or influences above doesn't make it a full-bodied wine. For example, Barolo is packed with tannin, Mosel Riesling is unashamedly sweet, while fino sherry comes in at 15% alcohol or more, yet none really qualifies for the term full-bodied. Full-flavoured, yes, full-bodied, no.

17 | does wine contain anything apart from grapes?

Bit of a can of worms this. Here are things that may have been added to your wine during production:-

Yeast. There are yeasts floating around in the air of both the vineyard and the winery. Some producers rely on these for their wines to ferment, others prefer to add them. And these added yeasts can have a profound influence on a wine's flavours, enhancing or suppressing particular aromas and flavours present in the grapes.

Yeast nutrients. If you suspect your yeast might struggle to complete the fermentation, you can add substances to spur it on its way.

Enzymes. Some of which help speed up extraction of flavours, while others enhance aromatic compounds.

Malolactic nutrients. We talked about MLF (malolactic fermentation) in the previous chapter. Winemakers can add these nutrients to speed up the process.

Sulphur. The winemaker's preservative, which can be added to a wine at several stages of wine production from harvesting to bottling. Its main use is to stop wines oxidising, but in sweet wines, it also inhibits yeast activity to make sure fermentation doesn't start up again. But don't blame it for headaches (see Chapter 95).

Sugar. In cooler parts of the world, sugar is added during fermentation to boost the final alcohol content.

Acid. In warmer climes, sugar is no problem, but lack of acidity is. So the winemaker adds what nature couldn't supply (and in places where there's too much acid, calcium carbonate is sometimes added to reduce the level).

Oak. Should we count an oak barrel as a wine additive? It certainly contributes to the flavour of a wine. Those who can't afford oak barrels can immerse barrel staves in their fermenting wine to give an oaky character. And if even that's too expensive, there are large tea-bag-like sachets of oak chips that can be suspended in the bubbling brew.

Clarification/Stabilisation agents. A newly-fermented wine is seldom crystal clear. Give it a long period of rest in tank or barrel and the floaters may all precipitate out, leaving a clear liquid, but even that isn't guaranteed. So to ensure clarity, and to speed up the process, several substances can be pressed into use. Dried blood (honestly) was once used, but has fallen from favour for some reason. However, animal-related products such as egg-whites, gelatine, casein (from milk) and isinglass (from – yes – fish bladders) are still common. Wines marked as suitable for vegetarians or vegans will often have been fined with bentonite, a form of clay.

Colour. Your wine isn't deep enough in colour for your liking? A scoop or two of a grape concentrate called Mega-Purple will make for something darker and steamier.

Tannin. Sometimes added for its preservative effect, but can also stabilise the colour of wines.

Water. If your wine's too strong, or you want to up production levels, just dilute it. But don't tell anyone, as it's illegal in many countries.

Alcohol. Usually not added to regular table wines, but a major ingredient in fortified wines – a typical port will be 80% wine and 20% added spirit.

MOG. Meaning Matter Other than Grapes. A term originating in those places where machine harvesting is common, and where the equipment picks up bits of trellising, leaves, branches, irrigation pipes, stones and occasionally small animals along with the grapes. With the improvement of machine harvesters, thankfully far less of this ends up at the winery than was once the case.

Hope that hasn't put you off! None of these substances is bad for you in the amounts used even in mass-market wines, and the good producers aim to work with as few of them as possible (read about Organic Wine in Chapter 9).

18 | are small independent wine producers going to survive in the next ten years?

The full question continued "...or are we going to suffer from mass-produced supermarket wines which are generally sh**?"

It's not going to be an either/or situation. Mass-produced supermarket wines are with us for the long haul. There will always be enough people who want a glass of wine/a slice of bread/a frozen chip without bothering too much about its origin and flavour. Sad but true, get used to it.

But independent wine producers are also not going away fast. However, whether it's going to be the SAME producers who survive from generation to generation is a different matter. Some of them will, but will remain small concerns, others will grow and merge with others and become larger businesses, while yet others will become complacent and go bust – with the void they leave then being filled by starry-eyed newcomers...

How? How? What?
Why? How? Who? What?
Who? How? What?
Why? When? where? When? How?
Why? When? How? Who? How?
what? How? Where?
When? When? Who?
When? When? Why?

Where? Who? When? What?
How? What? Who? When? How?
Who? How? When? Why? Why? How?
Who? What? Who? Who? Why? Why?
Who? Why? when? Where? Who?
What? What? How? How?
How? What? Why?
where? Where? What? Where? Who?

Who? When? What? How?
Who? Where?
Why? Who? Where? Who? Who? Where? What?
Why? What? When? Why? How?
Why? why? when? who? Why?
What? Where? Where? How? When?
Where? who?

How? When? Where?
What? Where? When?
Why? What? when? When? Why?
How? When? Who? How? How? Why?
Who? what? Why? What?
When? Who? Where? Where? When? How?
Why? Who? Where? How?

When? When?
Why? What? Who? When? what?
Who? Where? Where?
Why? How? Why? How?
Where? Who? when? Who? Why? How?
What? Where? Where? What? when?
How? When? Where?

When? When? What?
Where? What? How? Who? How? How?
Who? Why? Why? When? How? What? Where? Who? Why? where?
Where? Where? Why? When? What?
When? When? What?

I have a question about...

What Wine Is Made From

19-30

19 | can wine be made anywhere in the world?

The vast majority of vineyards lie in two bands 30° to 50° north and south of the Equator. Closer to the Equator, it's generally too warm, and often either too arid or too humid. Closer to the poles and it's too cold and/or wet.

However, there are exceptions. In northeast Brazil, you'll find vineyards at around 8-9°S, that are watered by the São Francisco river. As there's not much seasonal variation from month to month, the producers can control when the grapes grow through irrigation, and can even persuade the vines to produce two crops per year.

Staying in warm climes, there are vineyards in exotic places such as Madagascar, Thailand (look out for the Monsoon label) and Vietnam – Egyptian and Algerian wine seem positively mainstream in comparison. As in Brazil, some of these more equatorial vineyards are capable of yielding more than one crop a year, although often the producers prefer not to do this in order to avoid growing crops during the rainier times of the year.

At the opposite extreme, the burgeoning UK wine industry demonstrates that 50° is no longer the barrier it was once considered to be. Ireland, Belgium, Luxembourg and Holland are officially recognised by the EU as wine producing countries. Sweden too – the Blaxsta Vineyard at 59°N makes a range of wines from grapes and other fruit, and its Vidal Icewine has won medals in international competitions. However, it's pipped at the post for the title of the most northerly commercial vineyard by the Hallingstad Winery in Norway, location 60°N.

And further north still in Finland, a vineyard has been planted close to the Olkiluoto nuclear power station. Planted with the Zilga grape (no, I'm not familiar with it either), it survives thanks to underground pipes carrying warm water from the reactor cooling system. However, production is less than a tonne of grapes each year, so don't try and find the wine in the shops.

20 | why do wines from different places taste different?

Take a group of people, send them over to the other side of the world, and then examine them five generations later. What's happened? There'll be similarities with those people who stayed put, but there'll also be distinct differences. You could say that the new place had rubbed off on the travellers.

The same happens with grapes. Maybe once upon a time there was just one block of Syrah, but today the grape has travelled all over the world and become acclimatised to wherever it has settled. If its new home is warmer and sunnier than where it's come from, chances are that it will have developed slightly darker and thicker skin. If there's different vegetation surrounding the vineyards, then there'll be different aromatic oils wafting on the breeze and settling on the grapes. Syrah in France often has a whiff of the garrigue, the scrubby hillside vegetation made up of plants such as thyme, lavender, sage and rosemary. Syrah/Shiraz in Australia however is more likely to bear the aromatic stamp of eucalyptus trees.

There's also a human side to the difference in tastes from place to place. Wine is subject to the whims of fashion, just like many other topics. So some countries may like their Chardonnays crisp and lightly oaked, while others prefer them bold and barrel-y. Is one style "better" than the other? Not really, they're just different.

21 | how does climate affect the flavours of wine?

Hmm. Entire books are written on this topic, so trying to address it in a short space isn't going to be easy. But no matter, we'll set off and see where we get to...

Vines need light, heat and water in order to grow well. Too much or too little of each at the wrong times and they start to complain. Light and heat are related so let's look at them first, and let's talk about ripeness. Ever tried an unripe tomato? There are a few things you notice about it. Firstly, sweetness, or rather lack of it: this tomato is a sour puss. Then flavour. It feels pinched, lacking the piquancy of a fully ripe specimen. And finally appearance. If it had been allowed to ripen fully, it would eventually have become a lovely red tomato, but here, it's flecked with green.

You have here two aspects of ripeness that are much the same as with grapes, namely sugar ripeness and phenolic ripeness. Sugar ripeness comes about through photosynthesis, the process in which the plant converts light energy falling onto the leaves of the vine into sugar. The more sunlight and heat, the more sugar will end up in the grapes. Hand in hand with this is a corresponding fall in acidity, hence the tart character of our unripe tomato.

However, phenolic ripeness, which is the ripeness associated with colours and flavours (and tannin too), depends on sunlight falling on the grapes themselves.

This means that those growing their vines have to cultivate them in such a way that there are enough leaves for photosynthesis but not so many that the grapes are in the shade, nor so few that the grapes suffer from sunburn. And just as with humans and sun, there are different thresholds for what is just right and what is too much. White grapes in general need less than red, and even within those red ones, there's no such thing as an "ideal" amount: a variety such as Malbec can tolerate much more sun than Pinot Noir.

So coming back to the question, in an ideal climate, sugar ripening and phenolic ripening proceed at the same pace, resulting in a wine that has a reasonable amount of alcohol (thanks to the sugar), the right amount of acidity to keep it fresh, fully-developed but never overripe flavours and (if it's red) a level of tannin that's in balance with the rest of the wine. If the temperature is below ideal, there'll be less alcohol and more acidity, crisper flavours and maybe a slightly "green" edge to any tannin there. If it's *too* cool, then there'll be searing acidity with insufficient alcohol to flesh it out, plus an even greener, more bitter whack of tannin, through all of which any flavour in the wine will struggle to make its presence felt.

If however the climate is too warm, the grapegrower has a choice to make. Does he pick early, before the sugar has soared and the acidity dropped, but also before the flavours and tannins have fully developed? Or does he wait for phenolic ripeness, by which time the sugar will be sky-high, the acidity virtually non-existent and the grapes at risk of turning to raisins on the vine? Maybe the problem is that he's not growing the right grape varieties: as with sunlight, some grapes prefer the heat to others, and indeed need it in order to ripen fully. Which is why you don't see too much Grenache planted in northern Europe (although someone has planted some in Wales).

Got all that? Now let's make it even more complicated and bring in the diurnal swing, in other words the drop in the mercury from day to night. Many regions that at first seem to be too warm to grow grapes are actually able to because after baking hot days, the temperature drops dramatically when the sun goes down – for example Ribera del Duero in Spain typically experiences diurnal swings of 20°C or more.

A further temperature-related issue is frost. Over winter, vines are pretty hardy and can tolerate freezing temperatures. However once the growing season has started, frost is a deadly enemy, capable of literally nipping an entire year's crop in the bud in one night. Growers in some regions use gas or oil heaters in their vineyards to try and reduce its effect – although at around €4,000 per hectare per night, not all can afford this. Frost around harvest can also happen. If it's so severe that the leaves are damaged, then photosynthesis will stop, so the grapes need to be picked ASAP, even if they're not fully ripe.

Snow's not so much of an issue: if it's cold enough to snow regularly during the growing season, it's probably too cold for vines in the first place. But hail can be particularly nasty. In some regions you'll see the producers covering their vines with thick nets to spare them from the worst of its effects. When you see a hail-stricken vineyard with its shredded leaves and ravaged grapes, you understand why.

Now onto water. Vines need water to survive, but they don't want too much. The ideal is for the vines to get lots in the form of rain over the winter and early spring in order to swell the water table when the vines are dormant, and then a little over the rest of the season to stop them completely dehydrating, with none in the month or so prior to harvest. If there's too little, there's the option in many regions of augmenting what nature has provided with irrigation water – more about that in Chapter 29. If there's too much, there are two potential problems. Firstly, that the grapes will swell up and dilute the wine. Secondly, that the rain will be so vicious that it splits the grapes, making them susceptible to rot.

Speaking of rot, let's talk about humidity. Too much of it, especially in warm conditions, gives rise to rot and mildew. Most of the time, this is unwelcome, but there's one particular sort of rot called botrytis or noble rot that shrivels up the grapes, concentrating their flavours, and enabling the producers to make some exquisite sweet wine (read more about botrytis in Chapter 12). Very high levels of humidity and fog block the sunlight and moderate extremes of temperature. Many Californian vineyards would be too warm to grow grapes were it not for the fogs blowing off the cool Pacific Ocean.

Finally wind, which affects vines both positively and negatively. On the plus side, a good gust of warm wind after a period of rain can both prevent the spread of (unwanted) rot and blow away much of the excess moisture before it gets a chance to soak into the ground.

On the minus side, if it's too strong, it'll damage both leaves and grapes. And there's another aspect of how wind affects vineyards, but it's probably more appropriate to cover that in the next chapter.

22 | what effect do other natural factors have on a wine?

We've just touched on the effect climate has on a wine, but it's only one part of the impact the natural world can have on a wine. The French use the term "terroir" to describe the non-human properties of a particular piece of ground which affect the flavour of the ultimate wine – "sense of place" is as good a translation as any.

So what apart from climate and latitude (see earlier parts of this section) is involved in terroir?

Altitude. Generally, higher = cooler, although other factors can override this. So in the previous chapter, I mentioned the fog in California. In Napa Valley, some vineyards lie above the fog line, so they're actually warmer than those on the valley floor below.

Slope. The further you are from the equator, the lower the sun is in the sky. A vineyard inclined to face the midday sun will get more light and heat than one on the flat or pointing away from it. However there's also something called gravity to take into account. Put a big stone at the top of a hill and its inclination is to roll down. Put a load of very little stones – AKA soil – in the same situation and they'll tend to do the same. Which is why many vineyard owners spend a fair bit of time each year carrying topsoil from the bottom of a slope back up to the top. And why some vineyards contain other plants between the vines in order to bind the soil together. These are called cover crops: more about them, and soil, in a moment. But soil isn't the only thing that rolls down hills – water does too. Vineyards on steep slopes won't suck up as much rainwater as those on flatter ground. Which may or may not be a good thing. Related to slope is...

Aspect. In both hemispheres, the sun rises in the east and sets in the west. In a cool region, the best vineyards will be those on slopes that warm up soonest on chilly mornings and get a good dose of sun for as much of the rest of the day as possible. So in the northern hemisphere, they tend to face south to south east, while in the southern, it's north to north east. However in very warm places, the best vineyards for certain styles of wines may be those facing away from the midday sun. In the Douro valley in Portugal, many of the finest vineyards for port are south facing ones close to the river, so they benefit from both direct and reflected sunlight. But for white wines and some of the reds, the top sites are often the cooler ones high up on the opposite bank.

Proximity to water. As we saw above, reflected sunlight from a river can affect a vineyard. But large bodies of water like lakes and seas also act as heat sinks, cooling the vineyards in the heat of the day and warming them up when the sun has gone down. Sea breezes also bring with them salt in the air which can have an impact on the vines: many wines made close to the coast seem to have picked up a briny tang.

Soil. Vines are very clever things. There are instances of their root systems burrowing underground for several metres, and shimmying their way into the tiniest of crevices in the bedrock. However, especially when they have just been planted, they need some top soil a) for physical support, and b) from which to draw moisture and various nutrients.

If the climate is on the wet side, you want soil from which the rain drains away as quickly as possible, otherwise the vine roots will suck up too much moisture, resulting in grapes that are large but not very intense in flavour – quantity but not quality. Some vineyards will have cover crops (them again) to soak up some of the excess water. If conditions are very dry, you want the opposite, otherwise the grapes will either shrivel up or yield a crop too small to be economically viable.

Also, the flatter the terrain, generally the deeper and more fertile the topsoil. Fertility sounds like it should be a good thing, but while it makes for healthy looking vines and plump, happy grapes, again the result tends to more a case of quantity than quality. Conversely, the very steep slopes have the opposite problem: with hardly any top soil, not only will the vines struggle to get a foothold, but the yield will be tiny.

Finally, soil contains a variety of substances that affect how vines grow. The three most important elements are phosphorus, nitrogen and potassium, and ideally, the soil will provide some of each but not too much. Where nature is deficient, the grower has to either ring the fertiliser salesman or obtain the elements from more natural sources. Cover crops (yet again) can be grown and then ploughed into the soil to provide nitrogen especially, while manure can also be used sparingly.

But what is that soil actually made up of? Brace yourself for a crash course in wine geology, and for the introduction of THE ROCK CYCLE. No, it's not Wagner meets Van Halen, it's...complicated.

There are three basic type of rock, igneous, metamorphic and sedimentary. Igneous is formed when molten rock solidifies. Some igneous rocks like granite form under the earth's surface, while others (eg pumice and basalt) form when liquid rock hits the atmosphere, as with volcanoes.

Sedimentary rock is formed from (believe it or not) sediment. Sediment itself isn't a type of rock, but the result of the weathering and erosion of igneous and metamorphic rock into smaller pieces: clay, sand, gravel and so on. By some means – glaciers, floods, strong winds – these sediments end up being deposited in layers, and over the course of time, these layers solidify to become rocks such as sandstone, shale and limestone.

Metamorphic rock occurs when either sedimentary or igneous rock are subjected to high pressures (such as tectonic movements) and/or temperatures (in the earth's core), resulting in a change in composition. Examples include slate, marble and schist.

Got all that? So what effect does each have on wine style? Hmm... Some things are clear. Lighter coloured soils can reflect sunlight onto the vines but don't retain and then radiate the heat overnight, especially if the soil fragments are small. This can be useful in not-so-warm places with small diurnal swings (see previous chapter). Meanwhile darker soils that don't reflect the sun do retain and then radiate heat, especially in soil with larger stones, which can be useful in places where the nights are chilly.

But do the soils and the bedrock beneath them have an impact on actually flavour? Step forward "minerality", which deserves its own chapter...

23 | what is "minerality"?

Wine words are imprecise. A steely Chablis does not contain shards of shiny metal. A sparkling wine that smells of flowers and brioche doesn't have petals and blobs of dough floating on its surface. And that bold meaty southern Italian red isn't something that vegetarians need shy away from.

The term "minerality" has been used in wine circles for many years, but started rising in popularity from the late 1990s onwards. So what exactly is it?

The early answer was that if terroir was the factor that gave flavours in a wine that couldn't be attributed to grape variety, winemaking or weather, then minerality was the element of terroir influence resulting from the minerals present in the vineyard's soil. This explained why Rieslings from the slate-rich slopes of the Mosel often had a character reminiscent of wet slate roofs, and why Chardonnays from limestone soils had a seashell-like tang (and while minerality does crop up in tasting notes for red wines, it tends to be more common in whites, especially those with high acidity).

It sounds very plausible, but for a couple of things. Firstly, science has shown that there's no way that minerals in the soil could end up in the grapes themselves. Secondly, those minerals don't actually taste of anything in the first place. Also, winemakers have worked out that certain winemaking practices give rise to characteristics that many tasters lump under the heading of minerality.

What science HAS shown however is that the chemical composition of wine does vary from vineyard to vineyard. Moreover, when you taste through a range of whites from a producer in Burgundy, in which the winemaking is close to identical for each of the wines, there will be ones that come over all fleshy and fruity and others that are far more sleek and, well, minerally.

("Stony" might be a more useful term here. Ever licked a river pebble, or one on the beach? Ever smelt a slate roof after a storm? Ever been near a large outcrop of volcanic rock? No, the wines don't have pebbles, slate or lava in them, but nor do they have lemons, gooseberries, pineapples and other fruits that crop up in tasting notes.)

If it's not actual minerals being sucked up the roots, then what is it? Microbes could be to blame. The populations of microbes both above and below ground can never be identical from one site to the other. Those in the soil break down organic matter into substances the vine can use. Those in the air settle on the vines and affect the functioning of the various yeasts present.

In those vineyards that receive copious amounts of herbicides, fungicides and fertilisers, and where the wines are fermented with cultured yeasts, there's not going to be too much of a terroir imprint. Meanwhile at estates where the soil is healthy, and the fermentation kicks off thanks to the yeasts present in the air, then the site will give far more of a signature to the wine. But it'll be down to microbes, not minerals. Although the types of microbes may be influenced by the minerals in the soil...

24 | what effect is global warming having on wine?

A few points:-
- Alcohol levels are rising.
- Harvests are getting earlier, in some cases a month earlier than they were 50 years ago.
- Ways of managing vineyards are changing, as farmers attempt to slow down the rate at which their grapes ripen.
- Rainfall is more erratic – droughts then storms then back to droughts.
- In these conditions, soil erosion can be a problem in steeper vineyards.
- There's less water available for irrigation, so producers will have to be more inventive/frugal with the resources they have.
- Vineyards in some very hot regions are becoming unviable – there's just not enough water to sustain them.
- Many well-known regions may have to start looking at alternative grape varieties if they want to keep producing good wine.
- Places once considered unsuitable for vines are developing rapidly – the UK is a classic example.
- There may even be a need to rethink locations of forests for making oak barrels.

25 | what's the difference between different grape varieties?

First of all, let's establish what a grape variety is. Do you remember biological classification from school? The order runs Domain, Kingdom, Phylum, Class, Order, Family, Genus and Species. Vitis, the grapevine genus, is part of the Vitaceae family, and is split into several dozen species.

By far the most important of these is Vitis vinifera. Maybe once upon a time there was just one strain of vinifera. However, over the course of several millennia through a combination of natural means – cross-fertilisation, adaptation and mutation – and human influence – cultivating, breeding and crossing – we have arrived at the stage today where there are literally thousands of different varieties (if that was a bit too scientific, think of Granny Smith, Cox's Orange Pippin, Braeburn and Gala – all different varieties but all still apples).

Some grape varieties have been around so long that they're referred to as Founder Grape Varieties. These include Pinot, Cabernet Franc, Nebbiolo, Muscat, Savagnin (of which Gewürztraminer in a mutation) and Gouais Blanc. You may not have heard of Gouais Blanc but you will be familiar with some of its many offspring, such as Chardonnay, Gamay and Riesling.

Wine can be made from other Vitis species, and North Americans in particular will be familiar with Catawba and Concord, both varieties of Vitis labrusca. There are also hybrid grapes, created by crossing Vitis vinifera with other

Vitis species. These include Seyval Blanc, which is used for Sauvignon-esque whites in England for example, and Vidal, one of the main grapes used for Canadian Icewine.

However the greatest contribution of non-vinifera vines to the wine world is providing rootstocks for grafting. More of which in the next chapter.

26 | are vines better grafted or on original rootstock?

In the late 19th century, a bug called phylloxera vastatrix made its way across the Atlantic from America and proceeded to chomp its way through European vineyards, destroying Vitis vinifera vines as it went: France alone lost more than a million hectares of vines. The problem was only solved when scientists realised that the species of vines native to North America were immune to phylloxera. By grafting the vinifera shoots onto the roots of these other species, the vines were able to survive. The most common rootstocks today are hybrids from the riparia, rupestris and berlandieri species.

But do they have any effect on the wine quality? To this question, the answer is...unclear. The problem is that there are virtually no examples of wines made from grafted and ungrafted vines grown in the same way in the same vineyard and vinified identically with which to do a thorough comparison. In those places where grafting is the norm, those rare plots of vines on their own roots are likely to be lovingly tended by their owners. Could it be that the excellence of the wines is due to terroir and TLC rather than anything else?

(Not all vineyards succumbed to phylloxera. In Europe, pockets of ungrafted vines can still be found, such as on the steep slate slopes of the Mosel in Germany, or on the volcanic soils of Mount Etna. Elsewhere, places such as Chile, Washington State and large parts of Australia remain phylloxera-free, so ungrafted vines are common there.)

27 | how much wine does a vine produce?

There's no simple answer to this. Grape varieties vary in vigour, soils differ in fertility and grape growers differ in how they cultivate their vines. Do the vines receive a lot or a little water? And are they healthy? So for wines of comparative quality, in some countries the answer could be two bottles, while in others, it could be eight.

Let's look at extremes. At the lower end, each vine at Sauternes superstar Château d'Yquem yields just one glass of wine. At the upper end, in the more industrialised, heavily-irrigated vineyards around the world, a figure of two 12-bottle cases of wine per vine is not unheard of. Or to put it another way, one hundred and fifty times more wine per vine than at d'Yquem.

28 | is old vine wine better than young vine wine?

You may have seen the terms "Old Vines", or "Vieilles Vignes" or "Alte Reben" on bottles of wine. At the root of the question is whether it's worth paying the premium that these wines usually command. Vines are a bit like people. As they get older, maybe they're not as energetic and vigorous as they were in their youth, but (hopefully) the intensity of what they do increases. Quantity gives way to quality in other words.

Why? Well, much as with moving house, it takes time for the vines to settle into their new home, get to know the ins and outs of the neighbourhood, put their roots down. Those roots can take 20+ years to develop, and some say that it's only when they've grown to their full depth that the full impact of the terroir comes through in the grapes.

There's no formal definition of what makes an old vine. The only attempt at putting some sort of definition in place came from Australia's Yalumba and categorised the older vines of the Barossa Valley into four tiers: Old Vine (at least 35 years of age), Survivor (70+), Centenarian (100+) and Ancestor (125+)

But a question to pose to those who bang the Vieilles Vignes drum is one that I first heard asked by Phil Laffer, who spent years making Jacob's Creek into one of the world's most reliable wine brands. It is this: Is it actually old vines that make a wine great, or is it great wines that allow vines to get old? After all if the young vines had produced crappy wine, then wouldn't they have been ripped out and replaced with something else?

Consider 1961 Château Pétrus. In 1956, a devastating frost swept through Bordeaux and hit Pétrus as hard as any estate. Two-thirds of the vines were destroyed, and the remainder were regrafted. Meaning that one of the finest (and priciest – it's currently ~£5K a bottle) wines of the 20th century was made from five-year-old vines...

So yes, maybe older vines do tend to produce more intense wines than young ones. However, what is arguably more important to ultimate wine quality is having great terroir and an experienced grower who knows how to maximise its potential.

A related question is how long do grape vines last? There are examples of single vines that are over 200 years old, and South Australia has a number of commercial vineyards that date back to the 19th century. However, we need to remember that wine is a business. Unless they're able to command a significant premium for old vine fruit, most growers will uproot their less productive old vines and replant with more vigorous new ones as soon as economics dictates. Which in some vineyards could be after 60 years, and in others after only 30.

29 | is there any difference between wine from irrigated and unirrigated vines?

If vines receive insufficient water, they go into survival mode, shutting down the processes of growth and ripening. They live to fight another day (or another vintage) but the grapes they produce will not be very good. If they get too much water, they become the plant equivalent of couch potatoes, producing large amounts of grapes with inferior flavour.

So ideally irrigation should tread a line between these two extremes. But how it's used depends on the ambitions of the grapegrower. For some bulk wine producers, quantity is the important thing, so they'll turn the taps on and let the grapes plump up, hoping that they'll ripen sufficiently by the end of the growing season. At the opposite end of the quality spectrum, the goal is more likely to be to ensure the vine doesn't shut itself down but instead has enough moisture to survive and also enough vigour for its roots to start probing deeper underground for additional water reserves. Because if it finds these, there'll be less need for irrigation in the future.

So in some instances, irrigation makes for better wines, while in others, it makes for worse wines. And in larger quantities...

30 | which part of the world harvests first?

On January 1st, you may find grapes being picked in three very different situations.

1) Early. The bulk of the southern hemisphere grape harvest takes place from February through to May, but several vineyards in New South Wales in Australia for example are picked in January, and it's not unheard of for some grapes to be picked on New Year's Day.

2) Late. In the northern hemisphere, most grapes will have been picked by the end of November, but some producers looking to produce sweet Icewine will be harvesting well into December, and occasionally in January too (there's more about Icewine and other sweet wines in Chapter 9).

3) Whenever. As I mentioned in Chapter 19, the harvest in equatorial regions isn't governed by seasons. So each January 1st, there will be some vineyards in Thailand and northern Brazil that are being picked at optimum ripeness.

I have a question about...

Where Wine Comes From

31-34

31 | which are the most reliable wine regions in the world?

32 | where is the best value wine made?

33 | are the great wines of France still holding their own?

34 | what will be the Next Big Thing, the next "IT" wine?

31 | which are the most reliable wine regions in the world?

As in places where if you've never heard of the producer, you can still go ahead and pick the wine with reasonable confidence, regardless of price? These five were the first that sprang to mind...

Alsace, France. For the whites at least: the Pinot Noir can be good but it can also be scrawny. Otherwise this sheltered part of eastern France is a very happy hunting ground, as well as being a brilliant place for a holiday.

The Douro, Portugal. And I'm thinking here of table wines rather than the ports. Douro reds offer plenty of flavour but also freshness and something of the wildness of the rugged terrain. The rarer and surprisingly crisp whites are also worth seeking out.

Wachau, Austria. Riesling and Grüner Veltliner thrive on the steep slopes overlooking the Danube, and the air of healthy competition between the producers results in standards that are remarkably high. Neighbouring Kremstal and Kamptal aren't bad either.

Margaret River, Australia. A beautiful area that didn't suffer as much from the industrialisation of Australian wine in the 2000s as other parts of the country. Cabernet Sauvignon, Chardonnay and SSB – Semillon/Sauvignon Blanc blends – are the trump cards, but there's also remarkably good Riesling, Shiraz, Malbec and more.

Swartland, South Africa. There are some excellent old vineyards that are now being put to very good use. Chenin Blanc is the star white, but many wines include dollops of Viognier, Roussanne, Clairette, Chardonnay and whatever else the maverick producers in the region can get their mitts on. For reds, Shiraz is king, but Pinotage, Malbec, Mourvèdre, Cinsault and several other grapes are all being used to good effect.

32 | where is the best value wine made?

In a world of £80 Grand Cru Burgundies, a decent one costing £50 is great value. But I'm guessing you're thinking more of wines at the cheap end of the market. In which case, maybe it's best to speak from personal experience.

While my friends and family are (mostly) very nice, a lot of them aren't all that bothered about what goes down their throats. So I try to keep a stash of wines that I'd be very happy to drink, but which haven't cost an arm and a leg. Sorry independent wine merchants, I tend to pick these up from supermarkets.

So what do I buy? These usually feature...

Whites
Côtes de Gascogne/Saint Mont. Fresh pithy wines, many of them Sauvignon lookalikes, classic summer/seafood quaffers.
South African Chenin Blanc. Weighty and fruity, but with all the sunny apple, melon and honey flavours kept in check by zesty acidity.

Reds

Spanish Garnacha. Usually from Campo de Borja, also Calatayud, perfect spicy sausage-friendly midweek/barbecue gluggers.

Roussillon reds. There's lots of good value in southern France, but you seem to get a little more bang for your buck in Roussillon.

Portuguese reds. Both Tejo and Alentejo offer bags of fruit with a touch of wildness and a unique Portuguese accent.

Argentine Malbec. With its wealth of juicy dark berry flavour, this has taken over from Aussie Shiraz as the most reliable red of the southern hemisphere.

33 | are the great wines of France still holding their own?

With a few exceptions – Barolo & Brunello from Italy, Rioja and sherry from Spain, port from Portugal, Riesling from Germany – France provides the role model for the vast majority of wine styles that producers around the world seek to emulate. As for whether French wines are still the best, the answer is, "Yes but..."

What the globalisation of wine has brought about is an expansion of styles of wine, even within particular grape varieties. If you like the traditional, refreshing type of Cabernet Sauvignon, then Bordeaux is still top dog. If you want the bigger, bolder style, then Napa is king. With Syrah, hardly anywhere else achieves the combination of power and elegance found in the Rhône, but is it better than in its heart-warming South Australian form, or just different? And with Champagne, while the best wines have no equal anywhere in the world, at lower levels, there is serious competition from several places, among them Italy (for Franciacorta more than Prosecco), England, Spain (top Cava is seriously good) and Tasmania.

What France has certainly done over the last 30 years is lost its complacency. The good producers realise that a reputation has to be maintained and the result is a standard of wine that at its best is still world-beating. But while it is still the first port of call for many of those in search of great wine, it's no longer the only destination.

34 | what will be the Next Big Thing, the next "IT" wine?

This depends on whether you're talking about what will be the next darling of the wine world or what will appear from almost nowhere to colonise the supermarket shelves. Because there's precious little overlap.

In recent times, the first camp has included Austrian Grüner Veltliner, New-Wave California, En Rama Sherry, Orange Wine, Biodynamic Wine, Cru Beaujolais, Natural Wine, German Pinot Noir, Jura Wine, Growers' Champagne, Txakoli and Santorini Whites – there are probably more that I can't think of at the moment. What they all have in common is that at some point in the last 20 years, they have been for a time the darlings of many wine merchants and sommeliers in London and New York.

In the second camp, you have Australian Chardonnay and Shiraz, New Zealand Sauvignon Blanc, Argentine Malbec,

Pinot Grigio from almost anywhere, Prosecco, Blush and Fruit-flavoured wines.

Those who pursue the wines in the first camp often get very sniffy about those in the second, while those who lap up the wines in the second camp are usually unaware of those in the first.

Wouldn't it be great to have something that straddled both camps, the wine equivalent of David Attenborough's Planet Earth, Teenage Kicks or Tom Hanks? I'm struggling to think of one. The winos want individuality and are happy to find a bit of attitude, the general public wants value, consistency and no gawky bits.

Hence two lots of predictions, or at least two lots of hopes for the future...

WINOS
Jurançon. And other whites from South West France based on Petit and Gros Manseng. Their acidity take them out of crowd-pleaser territory, but their concentration, freshness, complexity and ageability are all to be admired, whether the wines are bone dry or decadently sweet.

Dão. There's a little of the "Here Be Dragons'" feel about this fascinating part of northern Portugal, and thanks to the typical vineyard holding of less than half a football pitch, there are hardly any really famous producers. However, in part thanks to the granite-rich soils, both reds, usually based on Touriga Nacional, and whites, where the main grape is Encruzado, have plenty of original things to say for themselves.

NORMAL PEOPLE

Chenin Blanc. Dry or sweet, still or sparkling, wooded or unwooded, fortified or unfortified, this versatile grape can do almost any style of white wine you'd care to mention. Its home is France's Loire Valley, but it's grown in many other places, with South Africa, California and Western Australia having sizeable plantings. If it can shake off its image as a workhorse grape in these places, its future looks bright.

Grenache. Surely the perfect grape for those parts of the New World that are proving too warm for Shiraz and Cabernet. Adept at making soft, friendly reds, but capable of a little more gravitas in the right places, it's at its best with a helping hand from other grapes to provide a little framework for its juicy flesh.

I have a question about...

Buying Wine

35-43

35 | how does a novice choose from 100s of bottles on the shelves?

Some ideas...

Mum knows best. Are there wines you remember being around when you were growing up? If so and you liked them, then buy the same. If you didn't like them, why not...

Phone a friend. What are your wine-loving friends or colleagues drinking? Most won't hold back if you ask for a few tips. Speaking of which...

Pressure of the press. In the papers, magazines and on social media, there's no shortage of people recommending wines. Try what they suggest and if you like it, stick with them. Otherwise find another guru, maybe from the press or maybe...

Ask the expert. Specialist shops of any kind can be daunting for the newbie, and wine shops are no exception, no matter what their proprietors say. But they're a great place to go both for advice and for the chance to try some of the bottles that many will have open for tastings, especially towards the weekend. And remember you don't have to visit a specialist shop to...

Experiment. You've found a Chilean Cabernet you like? Why not try the same producer's Merlot? Or a Cabernet from another Chilean producer? Or from a different country? Or a wine with Cabernet plus some other grapes?

And as you're working your way through these steps, try and work out whether there's a common thread to why you like some wines and dislike others. Take pictures to remind you of your favourites. Who knows, before long you may be the person novices come to for a few tips.

36 | why shouldn't I just drink the same wine all the time?

No reason at all. You won't die, you won't provoke general elections and you won't fall out with the neighbours if you stick to your old fave all the time. But do you eat the same meal every day? Or wear the same clothes? Or watch the same film? If you like wine – and I'm assuming you do, otherwise you wouldn't be reading this – then wouldn't you be interested in discovering a few more styles of wine to add to your list of favourites? So get out there, taste as many wines as possible and see if you can expand your wine repertoire. Otherwise there's a danger of FOMO – Fear Of Merlot Overload…

37 | why should I bother with any wine that's not on special offer?

Again, no reason. If wine is something that "bothers" you, just carry on with the banal, perpetually discounted, industrially produced and normally over-priced stuff that you currently buy, and leave the good stuff to those of us who like to drink something with a bit of personality.

(Having said that, I do sometimes buy from the January

sales that good wine merchants have, where quantities available are usually minuscule, and I also take advantage of those "25% off 6 bottles" offers that supermarkets often run.)

38 | is price an indicator of quality, or do some wines trade on their reputations?

Yes, and yes. Helpful that, I know, so let's unpack it.

It costs a certain amount to make a wine. Land has to be bought, vines have to be planted and tended. Grapes have to be picked and turned into wine, which then has to be sold (and often resold, sometimes twice), and profit has to be made by all those involved at the various stages.

Land that is capable of producing very good wine costs more than land where the produce is inferior, so that bumps the price up. But to maximise its potential, first of all you need to plant the finest vines – no point opting for Müller-Thurgau (the main grape in Liebfraumilch) when you're in classic Pinot Noir territory. Then to make the most of what's being grown, you need to employ the best grapegrowers and winemakers. And the best designers and marketers – you DO want your product to stand out from all the other high class wines available after all. Finally, you want to make sure you have a network of high-class importers in certain markets who will then place your wine in the "right" wine merchants and restaurants.

Settle for the cheapest at every stage of production and distribution, and you can just about crank out a wine that would sell in the UK at under £5 (of which close to 60% is duty and VAT, so adjust accordingly for different markets). Spare no expense and the price will be significantly higher. I reckon real personality in wine starts at around £10 a bottle, and (with a few exceptions) you'll have to pay at least twice that to get into blow-your-socks-off territory.

But when the quality of the raw materials and the standards of production are comparable, the reason why one wine sells for 2 or 3 times the price of one of similar quality is down to reputation. If the demand for a particular wine/producer/region outstrips the supply, then the price is going to rise. So mediocre red Burgundies cost more than vastly superior Chilean Pinot Noirs, and so-so Canadian Icewines sell for silly prices while many excellent sweet wines of South-West France struggle to find buyers.

And when you do find wines of the same standard at very different prices, you then have to decide whether it is worth paying extra for the reputation. This is not so much a qualitative decision as an emotional one. Drinking a prestigious bottle is similar to the experience of watching a legendary actor in a play, or eating at a renowned restaurant, or wearing an outfit by a famous designer, in that the reputation of the product adds to the pleasure of the experience. Anyone who's ever bought a new Apple product knows the satisfaction derived from simply unpacking it. No matter that an Android phone/Australian Cabernet of a similar standard might be significantly cheaper, if the iPhone/red Bordeaux makes you feel better, then you'll pay extra for it.

I'd advise anyone who is going to splash out on a great bottle to do so in the company of other wine lovers. The idea of going to "An Evening with Barbra Streisand" fills me with dread, and anyone who'd bought me a ticket for it would have wasted an awful lot of money. Similarly, if you have friends whose regular tipple is anything on special offer, make sure you hide that classy Barolo for another occasion. Maybe one where I'm invited...

39 | why do the British have to pay more for wine than they do in other parts of Europe?

(If you're not in the UK, skip this bit — I won't get huffy...)

The easiest way to answer this is to point you to an excellent 2015 piece from Gavin Quinney, a Brit who has been making wine in Bordeaux since 1999 – it's at bit.ly/gqduty.

The bottom line is duty. At the time of writing (Summer 2017), the duty on a 75cl bottle of wine sold in the UK is £2.16, which is then subject to VAT at 20%. Contrast this with Spain, where duty is zero, zilch, nothing, and VAT is 21% respectively. A huge difference which explains why that bottle of wine that is sold for £1 direct from a Spanish winery would cost a minimum of £3.58 on a UK shelf. And that's before any transport costs or profit margins for the importer and retailer have been added.

The message? Spend more on wine. Since duty is a flat rate, the proportion it makes up of the total cost of the bottle decreases, while that of the wine itself rises.

40 | where is the best place to buy wine?

Where's the best place to buy clothes? Or food? Different tastes, occasions, budgets and other factors mean that there's no one-size-fits-all wine merchant. So I'm going to split wine purchases according to a ranking that hopefully is self-explanatory: Wednesday, Friday, Payday. If you're a cheapskate, your Payday purchase might cost the same as (and maybe less than) what well-heeled winos would pay for their Wednesday wine, but I'm assuming here that you fall between these two extremes.

Wednesday Wines. Target price <£8/$12. The goal here is for something entertaining and tasty at a price that means you won't balk at adding a glassful or two from the bottle to the Spag Bol. Supermarkets are your friends here, and in the UK at least, the smart buys are the upmarket own-label wines (more on these in the next chapter). Otherwise look to some of the more wine-orientated chains of shops, although the choice here will be more limited. However, they come into their own when you get onto...

Friday Wines: Target price £8-£15/$12-25. The advantage of the wine chains is that there are often wines available to taste in store. Get to know the staff, and they'll inform you of new arrivals, small parcels of wine that may never make it onto the shelves and special events where you can try even more wine. This bracket is also where independent merchants become interesting. Some are brilliant, some are not. Again, take advantage of the tasting opportunities they offer and chat to the staff. If they're good, this could be the start of a beautiful relationship.

Mail order companies also have plenty of wines in this range, and while they don't have the advantage of being able to pop in for something for that evening, they often have large events at which you can taste your way through a large proportion of the range. But try not to get sucked in by the glossy marketing that some practise. All those half-price offers and money-off coupons off have to be paid for by someone, and it won't be the company itself...

Payday Wines: Target price £15/$25+. At this point, you're best off in the hands of an independent merchant. Or perhaps that should be merchants plural, since a merchant who specialises in Bordeaux might not be hot on Australian Chardonnay or Galician whites. And with online shopping, you now don't have to confine yourself to local stores. True, you'll often have to buy in larger quantities, but if it means getting a stash of special wines at the right price, that's no hardship.

As for finding these merchants in the first place, a quick search on Google combined with a few questions on social media should produce some candidates. And if you're in the UK, look for the companies that regularly perform well in competitions such as the International Wine Challenge and Decanter World Wine Awards.

(No, I haven't mentioned buying direct from the winery. It's a great way of stocking up, not least because you'll often find limited edition wines and may even get to speak to the winemaker. The best buys tend to be those from small wineries that don't make a large splash on export markets – at the famous estates, the wines aren't always cheaper than in the retail shops. However, the problem here is transport. If you like Chilean Cabernet, Austrian Riesling and South African Pinotage, you're going to have to spend rather a lot on travel and transportation to all three places in order to get the bottles back home...)

41 | are own-label wines good value?

Yes, no and maybe. Let me explain...

Supermarkets – and with own-label wines, they're the main operators in this niche – may want to take as much money off us as possible, but they also have a reputation to maintain. So when they put their name to a product, some thought has gone into it. They know that there are some people who will only buy the cheapest wine going. So they have a small range that caters for them. They know there are others who don't want to be seen as cheapskates, so they'll have the bulk of their range priced a step or two above. And they recognise that there are some who want something a little more ambitious, so there'll be some wines at a higher price point still.

And in general, you get what you pay for. The very cheapest will be at best OK, at worst undrinkable. Meanwhile the middle tier will be OK with a few gems and a few duds, while the upper tier will be better still, and the source of the best value wines in the range, even if they're the most expensive.

But there's another question: when is an own-label not an own-label? When it's a so-called "soft brand". A company has a wine made exclusively for them, but rather than slap its own name on them, it invents a new brand name and then sells it under that label. Because the wine isn't available anywhere else, the company can sell it for whatever price it thinks the market can stand. Soft brands are often offered at a high price and then discounted heavily, either on supermarket shelves or by mail-order/online wine companies as incentives to get people to sign up for their monthly offers. Buyer beware...

42 | this wine is covered in scores and medals – should I take any notice of them?

You get a medal for winning the gymnastics floor exercise at the Olympics. You also get one for growing the 3rd largest carrot at the village fête. Which is more impressive? Unless you're an ardent vegetable enthusiast, you'd go for the Olympic gong every time.

So it is with wines and medals. For any wine competition, or tasting at which medals or scores are awarded, you have to weigh up the depth and quality of the field, and the calibre of the judges. And their personal preferences: American palates tend to prefer bolder, riper, sweeter wines than European ones. Then you need to use your marketing bullshit detector – a £7 Cabernet may be very good, but if you really expect it to be "The Best Wine in the World", you're going to be disappointed. But if the wine makes it through those filters, then go for it.

43 | are there any good non-alcoholic wines?

With the honourable exceptions of the white Torres Natureo and Leitz's Eins Zwei Zero, virtually all others veer towards the grim (and they're not cheap either). Instead go for decent cordials, fruit juice diluted with sparkling water or just water itself. And a bottle of Angostura bitters is invaluable for livening up many drinks: yes, it's alcoholic, but a few dashes aren't going to disturb your sobriety.

(I posed a question about non-alcoholic wine on social media once, prompted by a question from my wife along the lines of, "Who drinks it?"

What was most disturbing of the replies from those who did was how they or someone they knew only drank it to try and kid people that they were actually having something more potent. "A Dad at school once told me he [drank it] for about a year. He had a heart condition, couldn't drink alcohol but didn't want it to be obvious." And another said, "I do sometimes...when I'm abstaining and don't want people to know."

Why? I'm not so much confused as disturbed. What is the problem with people seeing that you're not drinking alcohol? Do they think the wine police are going to follow them home and inject them with 15% alcohol Shiraz?)

I have a question about...

Wine Labels And Bottles

44-52

44 | why are wine bottles the colour, size and shape they are, and does this affect the wine?

Colour first. The more exposure to light the wine has, the faster it will age, becoming darker in colour and tasting less fresh. If the wine is stored in light-free conditions – if you keep it in the box, for example – then the glass colour is almost irrelevant. Once you let light get at the bottle, matters become a little more complicated. You'd think that darkest glass was best. And up to a point, you'd be right. However, darker objects also retain their heat longer than light ones. If ambient temperatures are really high, and the bottles never get a chance to cool down, then darkest is worst. Confused? Just keep your wine away from the light, and don't buy those bottles that look like they've been standing on bright shop shelves for weeks, even months on end.

Next, size. One theory as to why 750ml became the standard size is that this was the amount consumed at a typical 18th century meal: they were made of sterner stuff then – but then they also died earlier. Another is that this is roughly the capacity of a glass-blower's lungs.

But once this standard size had been adopted, smaller and larger formats emerged, usually some multiple or fraction of 750ml. And for some reason many are named after Biblical kings:- Half (0.375 litre); Bottle (0.75 l); Magnum (1.5 l); Jeroboam/Double Magnum (3 l); Rehoboam (4.5 l); Methuselah (6 l); Salmanazar (9 l); Balthazar (12 l); Nebuchadnezzar (15 l).

I've no idea who came up with the mnemonic to remember these of My Judy Really Makes Splendid Belching Noises – nor why they felt they needed it...

The larger the bottle, the less (proportionally) air it will contain, so the wine will mature more slowly. In other words, if you open a bottle and a magnum of the same wine, the magnum will be younger and fresher. Which could be good if it's an old wine, but the opposite of what you might want if it's a very young one.

Now the shape. The early bottles were often bulbous onion-like shapes, and the cylindrical form only developed with the growth in the glass industry, as traditional techniques such as glass blowing gave way to moulds. The new formats were easier to stack and transport, and also better suited for corks. There are four basic styles, perhaps best thought of as the wines most readily associated with each: Cabernet (straight sided), Chardonnay (more sloping shoulders), Riesling (taller and narrower) and Mateus Rosé (squat, round, table tennis bat-like). Do the different shapes affect the quality of the wine? No. Ditto for the depth of the indentation in the bottom of the bottle (known as the punt). Once upon a time, this was there to add strength and stability to the bottles, nowadays it's there for cosmetic effect.

The weight of the bottle gives a pointer towards the ambitions and aspirations of the producer. The theory goes that someone who puts some effort into the presentation of their wine will probably be doing the same in their vineyards and cellars. How something is presented makes a huge difference to how we perceive it, and wine is no exception to that. Bottles that stand out on the shelf get picked up off that shelf. Which is why there are now square bottles, triangular bottles, bottles with dimples, even bottles with a round bottom that come with their own special cradle.

45 | is there a problem with wine in plastic bottles or other packages?

This depends on how long the wine is actually going to be in the bottle. Or the Tetrapak, or the bag in box, or the can, or whatever. Many wines are now shipped in large tankers around the world and then packaged in the country where they're due to be sold. It makes perfect sense. Glass is heavy and fragile, and if you ship the wine in bulk you can get around three times as much into the equivalent space.*

However, glass is also far more inert and airtight than current plastics. So the longer a wine spends in a plastic bottle, the more at risk it is of both oxidation and being tainted by some of the chemicals leaching out of the bottle walls. As technology improves, these issues should diminish, but for the moment, plastic isn't quite as good a storage medium as glass. For wines that are destined to be sold within a few months of being bottled – and that's the vast majority of wines sold in these alternative packages – the effects should be unnoticeable. But for longer-term storage, glass is still the way to go.

* This gives rise to another question – how are wines affected by being shipped in bulk around the world rather

than being bottled where they were made? The tanker wine will probably end up being stabilised and filtered more often in order to protect it, so the wine with lose some personality and concentration with each process. But the cost saving and reduced carbon footprint make it a very attractive option.

46 | which is better, screwcap or cork?

It was in the year 2000 that a group of winemakers in Australia's Clare Valley decided to switch from natural corks to screwcaps for their Rieslings. The reasons were the incidence of bad corks (read about "corked" wine in Chapter 60), plus the way in which even good corks somehow stripped the aromatic elements of their wines. A couple of years later, their counterparts in Marlborough, New Zealand, did the same for their Sauvignon Blancs. Since then, both countries have embraced the screwcap cause to such an extent that anyone using natural cork is seen as a Luddite.

The impact of the screwcap elsewhere has varied. The UK has embraced it to such an extent that most people won't bat an eyelid when someone turns up for dinner with a screwcapped bottle. However in the US, it's still seen as the cheap option, regardless of the fact that many expensive wines now come with a screwcap rather than a cork. And in the wine-producing countries of Europe, especially in Spain & Portugal, home to more than 80% of the world's cork oak forests, cork still reigns.

But which is better? Hmm...

The original reasons those in Australia switched from cork was that too many bottles ended up not as they should be, either through cork taint (more of that in Chapter 60) or random oxidation, in which the seal wasn't as efficient as it should have been. Since then, the cork industry has pulled its socks up, much as Old World producers did when they realised that the threat from the New World wasn't going to go away. Today's corks are not perfect but they're cleaner and more reliable than they were.

As for screwcaps, their performance since 2000 has been good but not great. Yes, they keep wines tasting fresher for longer, which should be a bonus. However, there have been issues with the way in which some of the wines age. In particular, there are certain sulphur compounds in the wines that under screwcap become too pungent and prominent, but which don't develop in the bottles with corks (and this should come as no surprise: a wine aged in wood has a different character from one aged in the more inert environment of a stainless steel tank).

Which, along with the reluctance to embrace screwcaps in certain markets, is why a number of producers are switching back to natural cork. But let's not forget that while cork has centuries of use behind it, it's still early days for both the screwcap manufacturers and the winemakers who use their products. It may be that we see corks being used for certain styles of wines and screwcaps for others. Or it may not – which doesn't really answer the initial question, but is as good as I can do at the moment...

47 | how can I navigate my way through a wine label?

A quick glossary of the terms people ask about most frequently:-

Appellation. This deserves a chapter to itself, which just so happens to be the next one.

AVA. See the next chapter.

Barrique. The French name for a barrel that holds roughly 300 bottles of wine.

Brut. Term used for sparkling wine that is dry. Well, dry-ish – the scale of ascending sweetness runs Brut Nature, then Extra Brut, Brut, Extra Dry/Sec/Seco, Dry/Sec/Seco, Demi-Sec/Semi-Seco and finally Doux/Sweet/Dulce.

Château. French for "castle". And just as with Englishmen's homes, which are said to be their castles, some châteaux are spectacular and ornate, with wines to match, while others are glorified sheds – with wines to match...

Classico. Italian term used to denote the original heartland of a region – hence Chianti Classico, Soave Classico. Usually but not always the source of the best wines.

Clos. In France a vineyard surrounded by a wall, but the term is used more loosely elsewhere.

Contains Sulphites/Sulfites. Required on the label for legal reasons in many countries, but a pretty meaningless phrase — see Chapter 95 for why.

Côte(s)/Coteaux. French term meaning slope or slopes. If it's Coteaux, those slopes often overlook a river.

Crémant. Sparkling French wine that isn't from Champagne.

Crianza. Spanish term meaning "aged", as in the wine has spent some time both in barrel and bottle before the winery releases it. In Rioja for example, a Crianza will have spent a minimum of 12 months in both barrel and bottle. See Gran Reserva and Reserva.

Cru. A vineyard and sometimes a village considered to be of superior quality to others. Sometimes, there are crus that are considered of superior quality, in which case there'll be other words alongside Cru. For example, in Bordeaux (where the classification is actually of the producer, rather than their vineyards), you'll find Grand Cru Classé, Premier Cru Classé, Grand Cru, Cru Classé, Cru Bourgeois Supérieur and Cru Bourgeois Exceptionnel. Confused? Me too...

Cuvée. A batch of wine, often kept aside from the rest of production because it's superior or distinctly different.

DO(C)(G). See the next chapter.

Domaine. Estate.

Gran Reserva. Top of the tree in the Spanish aging hierarchy. In Rioja, the regulations are a minimum of 2 years in both barrel and bottle, and for the wine to be at least 5 years old before it's released. In other countries, it has no legal meaning.

Grand Cru. See Cru.

IGP/IGT. See the next chapter.

Late Harvest. A wine made from fruit harvested later than normal, resulting in the grapes having a higher sugar content. Usually, but not always, denotes a sweet wine.

Premier Cru. See Cru.

QmP/QbA. See the next chapter.

Reserva/Riserva/Reserve. Only has a legal definition in Spain and Italy: elsewhere, it's often slapped on bottles willy-nilly to try and impress people. In Spain, it's the level between Crianza and Gran Reserva: the requirements for a Rioja Reserva are nearly the same as for a Crianza except that the wine must be at least 3 years old before release. So in theory a wine could start life as a Crianza and become a Reserva a year later. In Italy, regulations differ from region to region, but most Riserva wines have to undergo a further year's aging beyond the requirements for the regular wine.

Sec/Seco/Secco. Dry. See Chapter 50.

Supérieur/ Superiore. Higher in alcohol than the normal wine, and hopefully superior in quality too.

Sur Lie. The lees – "lie" in French – are the yeasty deposits left over after fermentation has finished. The longer the finished wine remains in contact with these in the tank or barrel before it is bottled, the more it will pick up a yeasty, toasty, creamy edge.

Trocken/Halbtrocken. German terms meaning Dry and Off-Dry. Also see the next chapter.

VDQS. See the next chapter.

Vendange(s) Tardive(s). French for Late Harvest.

Vieilles Vignes. Old Vines. See Chapter 28.

Vin de France/Pays/Table. See the next chapter.

Vintage. See Chapter 51.

48 | what does Appellation Contrôlée mean?

Pull up a chair. Correction. Pour yourself a large glass of wine, then pull up a chair. This isn't going to be the most interesting answer in the book, but once you get your head round the concepts, you won't need to think too much about them again. Apart from with Germany...

Most European wine-producing countries have a system of regulating wine (and cheese and meat and other things) according to its origin and method of production. The most recent legislation splits these into PDO (Protected Designation of Origin) and PGI (Protected Geographical Indication), with the regulations for PDO being stricter than those for PGI. So a wine made from traditional local grapes and produced in a certain way might carry a PDO, while one made with higher yields (see Chapter 16) and non-native grapes would be a PGI. But is there a Europe-wide terminology for these designations? Hmm, no...

France

The PDO here is called Appellation d'Origine Protégée (AOP). The old name Appellation d'Origine Contrôlée (AOC) should have been phased out by now, but it's still very much around. The PGI used to be known as Vin de Pays, but is now Indication Géographique Protégée (IGP). There's also a slightly weird category called VDQS (Vin Délimité de Qualité Supérieure) made up of wines which should by now have been moved to either AOP or IGP, but that are still waiting. And finally there's Vin de France, introduced to replace Vin de Table in 2010. The labels don't say where the wine is from, but they can bear its vintage and grape variety, something that was forbidden with Vin de Table.

Spain

Denominación de Origen (DO) is the PDO, and there's a higher level of DOC for Rioja (C for Calificada) and DOQ in Catalan-speaking Priorat (Q for Qualificada). Vino de la Tierra is the PGI equivalent, and there's Vino de Mesa for basic table wine. In addition, there's Vinos de Calidad con Indicacion Geografica (VCIG), which roughly equates to France's VDQS, and Vino de Pago, recognising a single estate (pago) that makes wines of a very high standard.

Italy

The system is reasonably similar to that of Spain, with Denominazione di Origine Controllata (DOC) being the PDO, plus the (allegedly) higher level DOCG (e Garantita). PGI here is known as Indicazione Geografica Tipica (IGT) – many of Italy's top wines fall into this category – while base of the quality pyramid is Vino da Tavola.

Portugal

It's getting a bit easier now. Denominação de Origem Controlada (DOC) is the PDO, Vinho Regional (VR) is the PGI and Indicação de Proveniência Regulamentada (IPR) is the VDQS equivalent.

Germany

Did I say it was getting easier? Strike that. Germany splits its wines into four categories, Deutscher Tafelwein (Table Wine), Deutscher Landwein (Superior Table Wine), Qualitätswein bestimmter Anbaugebiete (QbA), meaning quality wine from a specific region, and top of the tree Qualitätswein mit Prädikat (QmP), meaning quality wine of superior quality.

It then subdivides QmP wines into six further bands, based on the ripeness of the grapes at harvest. The scale goes Kabinett (lightest), Spätlese, Auslese, Beerenauslese and Trockenbeerenauslese (sweetest), with the sixth category being Eiswein, which is made from grapes that are allowed to freeze on the vine prior to harvest.

To make things "simpler", it often adds extra designations to the labels, such as Trocken (dry), Halbtrocken (off-dry) and Feinherb (usually slightly sweeter than halbtrocken). And prompted by a surge in their popularity in recent years, the dry wines are now split into three classes, Classic, Selection and Erstes Gewächs (meaning first growths), with this latter being from sites that are deemed the best in the Rheingau.

Yes, this top classification is currently just for the Rheingau, which has prompted growers elsewhere to come up with their own as yet unofficial alternatives in the form of Großes Gewächs (great growths) and Erste Lagen (first class sites). But there's currently debate about whether these should just be for dry wines or sweeter ones too... My experience is that as soon as you've got your head around German wine laws, they'll introduce another one just to keep you on your toes.

These are the main ones you'll come across, and certainly potentially the most confusing. Outside Europe, many wine regions do have wine laws of differing levels of stringency. Depending on where you are, a minimum of 75-95% of the wine must be from the vintage, region and grape variety stated on the label. The USA has American Viticultural Areas (AVAs), but these only govern the source of the grapes, not which grapes are used, nor the method of production.

49 | why are some wines labelled by origin and others by grape variety?

Once upon a time, people didn't used to travel very far from their birthplace, and the same was true for wine. So the situation would arise where you had adjacent villages, both making wines from a similar mix of local grapes. Hardly anyone was bothered what those grapes actually were: they were just the varieties that had grown well there for generations – those that didn't grow well would have been abandoned long ago. How did you differentiate between the wines from the two villages? By calling them by those villages' names. Hence the traditional European/ Old World way of labelling wines geographically.

When New World producers began to plant vineyards, they didn't have those centuries of experience to show which grapes performed well in which vineyards. Many took a scattergun approach, planting cuttings from vineyards throughout Europe, and France in particular. Not all of them proved suitable, but many thrived, and the result was wineries with a large selection of both reds and whites. How were you to differentiate between wines grown in the same locality, but that were quite different in style? By grape variety.

I often get the line, "Why don't the French put grape varieties on their labels." So I ask them whether they mind not having grapes listed on bottles of port, Champagne and Rioja. They usually go quiet. Those coming at the topic from an Old World point of view often trot out the line about how all Australian wines (or those of any other non-European country) taste the same. So you put two Chardonnays in front of them, one from Tasmania, one from McLaren Vale. Grudgingly, they modify their view to MOST Australian wines tasting the same...

In an ideal world, modern wines would be labelled to include both geographical and varietal information, along with a back label that gives some sort of guidance as to the style of the wine. Plus of course the name of the producer, which is arguably more important than both.

50 | what is a "dry" wine?

A simple question, a not-so-simple answer. When it comes to wine labels, dry is at one end of the scale, and sweet is at the other, with medium dry and medium in between.

There are regulations regarding the levels of residual sugar (RS, measured in grams per litre) a wine can have in order to qualify for each category.

That seems simple enough. What isn't so simple is the way in which people perceive dryness and sweetness in wine. Let's talk apples for a moment, and in particular Granny Smiths, Coxes and Golden Delicious. There's not too much difference in the amount of sweetness each of them has, but there's a big difference in the amount of tartness AKA acidity. Hence the (sharp) Granny Smith seeming much less sweet than the (soft) Golden Delicious, with the Cox sitting in the middle. So it is with grapes. Some varieties are naturally higher in acid than others, and grapes grown in cooler climates are generally higher in acid than those from warm places. Hence a cool-climate Riesling with 10 g/l RS will seem drier than a warm-climate Muscat with less than half that amount.

Then you have to factor in tannin (more of which in Chapter 21). The higher the level of tannin, the drier and more astringent the wine will seem. Which is why Grenache, a grape low in both acidity and tannin, is generally on the soft, gentle side, and often produces wines that, though "dry" in sugar terms, can appear sweet alongside a high tannin Cabernet Sauvignon with the same RS level.

51 | what does "vintage" mean?

First, what it does NOT mean, at least where wine is concerned. It does not mean good and it does not mean old. It simply denotes the year in which the grapes were picked (or at least the majority of them: regulations permit growers in some parts of the world to include as much as 25% of wine from other years in the blend).

So why has "vintage" become synonymous for some people with quality? Blame the weather. In all but a few vineyards around the world, there is just one harvest each year. Sometimes the weather is great, and that year's wine is correspondingly great. Sometimes, nature is not so friendly, and the wine suffers.

In order to compensate for this, producers in some regions blend lesser years with better ones, in order to maintain consistency. The result is a non-vintage (NV) wine. But in those good years, they'll also keep hold of some of the best batches of wine and bottle them separately. That's a vintage wine. Vintage port and vintage Champagne are the two most common instances of this, and in these instances, you could say that "vintage" denotes quality. But otherwise, "vintage" just means the year the grapes were harvested, no more, no less.

52 | how much notice should I take of the year on a bottle?

There are two factors to consider. Firstly, you sometimes want the vintage to know how old a wine is. With certain wines, DYA – Drink Youngest Available – is the best advice. Sauvignon Blanc and Pinot Grigio aren't poisonous when they're five years old, but they'll hardly be gushing with youthful appeal. With others, the opposite is true. Very young, tough red wines may be drinkable, but that doesn't mean they'll be enjoyable. Finding something that's a little older and more mellow is advisable in such instances.

Secondly, there's the issue of how weather conditions vary from one year to the next. In some regions, generally the warmer, drier ones, one vintage isn't vastly different from the next. In others, that difference can be huge – ask anyone who has been on seaside holidays in northern Europe. Generally the further you get from the Equator, the more important it is to take notice of vintages.

Two codas to this last point. Don't make the mistake of thinking that because it was a good vintage in Region X, it was also good in Region Y. And don't forget that the best winemakers are still going to make something decent in less than stellar vintages. Think of it this way: would you rather have a meal made by a poor chef from great ingredients or by a great chef from poor ingredients? I'd take the second one every time. In other words, you'll be better served remembering a list of good producers than one of good, bad and ugly vintages.

I have a question about...

Tasting Wine

53-64

53 | do I need to do all that swirling and sniffing?

Just as some people never shut up from the moment you meet them, certain wines leap out of your glass without any need for swirling and swishing. But others (just like some people) need a little coaxing to reveal their true selves. So shake that glass, allow the wine to come out of its shell and you may be pleasantly surprised. Or you may not be – not all wines (or people) are packed with personality...

As for the sniffing, have you ever said when some food's brought to the table, "Mmm, that smells delicious"? Did it add to the pleasure of the meal? Most certainly. Most of our taste receptors are in our noses rather than on our tongues, which is why food tastes more bland when you have a cold. I'm not suggesting pour the wine up your left nostril, but do at least give it a good sniff (after a swirl). It'll increase the pleasure you get out of each bottle.

54 | can I tell anything about a wine by its appearance?

Quite a bit. Reds first. Young reds are vibrant purple or ruby, older ones have acquired tinges of brown, and may have traces of sediment in the bottom of the bottle (see Chapter 75). A deeper, darker colour doesn't necessarily mean more depth of flavour. Some grapes have naturally paler skins than others, so for example Malbec and Cabernet Sauvignon are much darker-skinned than Pinot Noir and Nebbiolo.

However, if you have two Cabernets of similar origin and one is much darker than the other, it could be one of two things. Firstly, the grapes could be smaller with the darker one. The smaller the grapes, the higher the ratio of grapeskin to grape juice, so the deeper in colour, flavour and tannin the wine will be. Or secondly, remember the tea bit from Chapter 7? Longer maceration also leads to wines with extra colour, flavour and tannin.

With whites, younger wines tend to be pale and can even have hints of green. With time, or after several months in an oak barrel (more about oak in Chapter 8), they become more golden and then, as with the reds, begin to turn brown. Again, some grapes have more pigment than others: Pinot Grigio and Gewürztraminer for example have pink skins come harvest time.

The last thing you can tell from a wine's appearance relates to alcoholic strength. In a wine with higher alcohol, "legs" or "tears" cling to the side of the glass longer after you've swirled it. They're not a sign of quality, just that the wine isn't going to be shy in the potency department.

55 | why do wines taste like strawberries or peaches or blackberries if they're only made from grapes?

Grape juice tastes of grapes. Fermented grape juice tastes of... You only have to look through some wine tasting notes to see that grapes are low down the list of descriptors. It's due to fermentation. During this process, not only is sugar converted to alcohol but also various compounds are produced, many of which are exactly the same as those found in other fruits. And vegetables. And flowers. And herbs and spices. And cat pee. And in those strange drawer liners your gran used to have.

There are other flavours in wines that are the consequence of the way they've been made. Wood aging can give characteristics of coffee, chocolate, vanilla and various spices. Lees aging – leaving the wine on the post-fermentation sludge for a period – adds yeasty overtones, as well as nutty oatmeal and cream notes. Malolactic fermentation, in which hard, apple-like malic acid present in the grapes is converted into softer lactic acid, can add a hint of butter. Exposing the wine to oxygen adds one type of flavour; excluding it completely adds a different one. Strains of bacteria and yeast in the air in the winery contribute yet more. Hence the many non-grapey flavours.

56 | why can't I smell all those blackberries and wet dog that they seem to do on TV?

The previous chapter looked at how it's possible for various blackberry-like or canine characters to appear in a wine. Whether you detect them or not is a different matter. Have you ever heard a piece of music for the first time, and it's reminded you of something else? And then have you had the experience of trying to explain that to another person only for them to look at you blankly?

It's similar with wine – some people just spend a lot of time sniffing odd fruits and dogs, so when there's a similar aroma in a wine, they'll notice it more. Also some tongues just have more taste buds than others. If you can't detect what others say they can, don't get hung up about it.

But maybe next time you have two glasses of different wines side by side, start thinking about how they're different. Is one softer, or sweeter, or chewier, or fruitier, or more potent than the other? The question of whether it's blackberry or blackcurrant can wait, just start simple.

57 | this wine tastes bad – why?

You're going to have to expand on badness here. Could one of these be to blame?

1) "It chewy and makes my mouth fur up." See Chapter 58.
2) "It's buttock-clenchingly tart." See Chapter 59
3) "It smells of musty cupboards." See Chapter 60
4) "It seems flat and tired, like bad old sherry." It's oxidised, meaning that too much air has got into it at some point in its life. A bad cork may be to blame, or you could just have kept that bottle too long.
5) "It smells like horse blankets and/or bandages." That could be brett (short for brettanomyces), a strain of yeast that in small doses can add a little character to some wines but in larger amounts mutes fresh fruit flavour, and makes any rough tannins poke out.
6) "It's vinegar-y." Volatile acidity (VA) is to blame here. As with brett, a hint of it can actually be pleasant, but in large amounts, it's actively nasty.

7) "It smells like rotten eggs." That's hydrogen sulphide, which develops naturally in winemaking. Good producers spot it ASAP and eliminate it. Bad ones sadly don't...

8) "I can't put my finger on it, it's just not nice." There are far fewer bad wines out there than once was the case, but you'll still find them. Just remember what the wine was and avoid it next time. And if it was recommended by a wine merchant, take it back (with most of the contents still intact) and you should get a replacement.

58 | why does this wine dry my mouth out so much?

Tannin is the substance that's to blame for making a wine chewy and bitter, and for drying your mouth out. Most of the time, it comes from grapeskins, but it's also found in oak barrels, and some winemakers actually add it in powdered form to their wines as a preservative.

Some people love that chewy character in their wine. But many don't, even if it doesn't give them a headache (see Chapter 95). What should they do? Some pointers...

1) Don't serve your red wines too cold. Ever noticed how the cup of tea that tastes fine when it's hot becomes bitter and astringent when it's cold? It's the same with red wine.

2) Drink red wine with protein-rich foods. When red wine turns your mouth dry, it's because the tannin latches on to the proteins in your saliva, making it less slippery. If there's protein from food around, it can latch on to that instead.

3) Stay away from high-tannin grapes such as Cabernet Sauvignon, Nebbiolo and Tempranillo in favour of low-tannin ones like Grenache, Merlot and Pinot Noir.

4) Look for wines from warm countries/regions. Wines from warm (not hot) places tend to have the softest, friendliest tannins (it's to do with phenolic ripeness – read more about that in Chapter 21).

5) Seek out older wines. Tannins are chains of molecules and over time, they link together and fall to the bottom of the barrel or bottle, leaving the wine softer and smoother.

59 | this wine is tart – why?

It's acidity that's making your mouth pucker and your buttocks clench. And while all wines are acidic – for the chemically inclined, they fall between 2.9 and 4 on the pH scale – there are some where that acidity pokes out more than in others, especially whites.

In general, the lower the pH, the tarter the wine will appear. However, it's not an absolute rule of thumb. Think of the acidity as a skeleton. The more flesh there is on that skeleton, in the form of flavour, alcohol and sugar, the less bony the wine will appear. And with wine as with people, everyone has their different idea of what is the right amount of flesh on that skeleton.

If you're not a fan of acidity, if you're not one of those people who chew their lemons when you have a gin and tonic, there are some steps you can take to avoid the incidence of pucker.

1) Stick to wines from warmer countries, as they generally have lower acidity levels (see chapter 21 for why).

2) Don't overchill your wines, as this heightens the acidity.

3) Save wines that you find a little sharp for mealtimes –
which is often when they were intended to be drunk.
4) Choose lower acid grapes such as Chardonnay, Pinot
Grigio and Viognier rather than Riesling and Chenin Blanc.

60 | what is "corked" wine?

Chemistry time. TCA (2,4,6-trichloroanisole if you can spell
and/or pronounce it) is a compound that occurs naturally
when fungi and bacteria in the air combine with chlorine-
based compounds (it has a close friend 2,4,6-
tribromoanisole – TBA – in which bromine is involved).

Wine problems begin when those chlorine products are
involved in wood production – pesticides, fungicides,
disinfectants and so on – and the affected wood then
comes into contact with the wine. The impact can be
drastic. In small doses, the wine won't be actively nasty,
but its flavours and aromas will have been diminished. In
larger doses, it gives a horrible, dank, musty character.

Most of the time, the culprit is the cork, hence the term
"corked", or cork taint. However, oak barrels, storage
pallets and even the wooden beams of wineries can
become affected. Some producers have had to destroy
their cellar and build a new one from scratch in order to
eliminate TCA.

Is there anything you can do to rescue corked wine? Some
people swear by adding a rolled up ball of polythene-based
cling film to a decanter full of the offending wine. In my
experience, while this seems to diminish some of the
mustiness, it doesn't restore the flavours that the cork

taint has stripped from the wine. Which is why many producers now use alternative closures for their wine bottles (see Chapter 46).

61 | do critics prefer certain wines to punters?

What good critics have in comparison with normal wine drinkers is deeper and broader experience. They can look at a young wine and judge it not only on how it tastes today but on what's going to happen to it in the future. They can think of how a wine that by itself is a bit tart and/or tannic would taste delicious with some food. And they're not seduced by gym bunny wines, wines that wave their immediate charms – ripeness, sweetness, oak, alcohol – in your face but don't have much personality beyond that.

Which is why every few months, there's a story of someone taking a popular cheap wine and a rare expensive wine – usually a young one – down to the railway station to do a comparative tasting. Invariably, the cheap one comes out on top. And this shouldn't come as any surprise – Dan Brown books, One Direction albums and Adam Sandler films seldom make the critics' choices, but that doesn't seem to affect their popularity.

The important thing for wine critics is not to lose touch with what normal people are drinking. If we can point those people who are interested – and not everyone is – in the direction of something similar but more inspiring, then that's a job well done.

62 | do women make better wine tasters than men?

Historically, knowing stuff about wine has been a male preserve. There's something about the subject that appeals to the nerd in men. They fill their heads with lists of grand cru vineyards and top vintages, much as they do with football scores and information on the latest Mercedes or Lexus. They're the ones who memorise which wines were awarded 95 points by the Wine Spectator, and whether the 2010 vintage of Château X contained 47% or 45% Merlot. And they're not afraid to share their knowledge with anyone willing to listen.

However, do males & females prefer different wines? No. The myth arises because in M-F couples where one of them is really into wine and the other just likes drinking it, it's usually the male who has the copies of Decanter stacked up on his side of the bed. In this case, yes, their tastes will differ. But if they have the same level of enthusiasm and experience, and don't succumb to peer pressure, then any differences will be down to personal preferences rather than being gender-related.

But never mind that, the question is do women make better wine tasters than men? The current science actually suggests the opposite. Our ability to taste wines, and indeed anything else, is apparently determined solely by the number of taste buds on our tongues and scent receptors in our noses. Researchers have discovered not only that people fall into three broad categories – non-tasters, normal tasters and super-tasters – but also that of the quarter of the population who fall into the super-taster bracket, nearly 80% are women.

Moreover, many women find that when they're pregnant, their senses of smell and taste seem to go into overdrive, especially during the early months. One UK supermarket considered recruiting pregnant women to help them in the wine department, based on the experiences of their buying team – at one point, four of them were all expectant mothers!

And it's certainly fair to say that women use their noses in everyday life more than men. Even today, they are usually the ones who spend more time buying and preparing food. They're more interested in perfume and fragrances, and tend to detect the whiff of an iffy nappy well before their male counterparts.

So is all hope lost for men as wine tasters? Not quite. Nature may have dealt females a better hand, but men can still call on their memory banks to put flavours in a wine into context. And with less space allocated to aromas of children, food and fragrances, they have more room for filing away wine experiences. So while a woman might say, "It smells of almonds and peaches," a man might say, "This reminds me of that white Burgundy from Domaine Sauzet we had last year."

One female Master of Wine put it like this: "Men are good at describing what I call the 'bones' of a wine – body, tannin, structure and length. Women talk about real flavours and aroma, so we help to put flesh on those bones. We evolved this way; many years ago the women were the ones who learned to taste in a sensitive way, making sure we weren't going to poison the village!"

63 | does wine taste different when we get older?

A couple of factors are involved here. One is how our personal tastes change. At 50, you usually don't wear/drive/frequent the same clothes/car/clubs you did when you were 25, and it's the same with wine. We move on, we evolve, we develop. Chances are that the wines that first made an impression on you were one of three things. Firstly, sweet: as Mary Poppins (nearly) said, a spoonful of sugar helps the Madiran go down. A touch of sweetness makes wines with obvious tannin and/or acidity a little more user friendly. Secondly, loud: big, jammy, almost port-like reds, bold, often oaky whites that shamelessly waggle their tropical fruit flavours under your nose. Thirdly, bland: pale in colour, pale in character, inoffensive but instantly forgettable, the liquid equivalent of lift music and rice crackers.

Let's be honest here. An awful lot of people don't budge much over the course of their drinking life. But enough of the population does, otherwise I'd be out of a job. Those of us who do move on get used to tannin and acidity, and start to seek out wines that lie between the extremes of too brash and too quiet.

But alongside the evolution of our tastes in wine is a physiological change. From the age of around 45 – slightly lower for women and higher for men – the rate at which our tastebuds are regenerated seems to slow down. Also, we can have diseases and undergo treatments that mute our senses of smell and taste. The result is that wines and foods that we used to enjoy can start to appear a little bland. Do you have any older relatives who insist on adding what you think is way too much salt or sugar to their food? This is why.

Can we do anything to counter this? Not really. However, while a 60-year-old will never recapture the physique she had forty years earlier, she will still be able to look after what is left. So be kind to your tastebuds. Get lots of fresh air and drink lots of water to clean your tongue, clear out your nasal cavities and moisten your mucus membranes. When you're drinking a wine, think of its appearance and texture. And keep your tongue and nose on their toes by not sticking to the same old wines week after week.

64 | this wine doesn't taste as good as it did on holiday – why?

Strange isn't it how something you last enjoyed in the company of your significant other on a golden beach by an azure sea while feasting on salted almonds/fresh garlic prawns/your significant other seems slightly different on a wet and windy night in Birmingham...

Very occasionally, it may be the wine that is at fault. Like some people, certain wines take days to recover from long journeys. In such instances, let them be for another week or so, and then try them again. But if they've still not improved, then chances are you were swayed by your surroundings. All you can do is send your significant other out to the shop for something more palatable.

I have a question about...

Keeping Wine

65-71

65 | should I lay some wine down for when my (god-) son/daughter turns 18?

66 | what's the best wine to buy as a present?

67 | is it worth investing in wine?

68 | how long does wine last?

69 | this one is older than that one - does that mean it's better?

70 | how can you spot a wine that will age well?

71 | how should I store my wine?

65 | should I lay some wine down for when my (god-) son/daughter turns 18?

I'm in two minds here. The wino in me says that anyone would be overwhelmed with gratitude to receive a case of something mature and tasty as they pass into adulthood. But another bit of me says, "Whoa, whoa, hang on a minute, squire." It asks me what I would have done had I been presented with a dozen bottles of grog on my 18th.

Yes, I drank wine then, but I don't think I'd have been too bothered which vintage it was from, as long as it didn't make me go blind. I seriously doubt whether any would have been left a week later. Maybe even a weekend later...

It then starts asking me whether I wouldn't be better off investing the money until a much later date when it became clear whether or not little Topsy/Tim actually enjoyed wine. If they didn't, then I could buy something else. If they did, then I'd have a larger kitty to play with. Yes, some wines do rise in value over time, but the ones that do are usually seriously expensive to begin with.

Then there's the problem of storing the stuff. If you don't have suitable space, you have to factor in professional storage charges, currently ~£12 per case per year. Even if you do, you still have to make sure that the stash is safe from prying hands – and not just those of devious adolescents. Many wine lovers have tales of how they "accidentally" opened that precious bottle of Château l'Aisselle de Singe in the wee small hours long after their taste buds and sensibility had retired to bed.

Two more thoughts. Thanks to better grape-growing and winemaking, gone are the days when you NEEDED to keep some wines in order for them to be drinkable. And finally, I have a sneaky suspicion about many (as in many, not all...) old wines. It is that beyond a certain point, they start to taste rather similar. Soft, mellow and hopefully still fruity, but with not much imprint of their place of birth. Most wines taste different at age 21 than they did at 10, but how many of them are actually better?

That's another reason that – for the moment at least – tips me in favour of hanging onto the money rather than forking out at birth. That way, when Johnny/Joanna comes of age, you can buy some younger wines and maybe chuck in a lone bottle (vintage port will go the distance) you've kept from his/her birth year. That is if it hasn't "accidentally" been opened already...

66 | what's the best wine to buy as a present?

If they're a good friend, then you're more likely to know the types of wines they do and don't like. If not, there's still a decent chance that they'll like those perennial favourites sparkling wine (at any time of the year) and port (coming up to Christmas).

In either case, set your budget then head to a good local wine merchant and tell them what you're looking for. Supermarkets should be your last resort and if you do have to use one, don't buy a wine that's on a half-price offer unless you want to be known as a cheapskate.

Is that too vague? If so, might as well say that if anyone turned up at my house with a bottle of Pol Roger NV or virtually any 20 Year Old Tawny Port, they'd almost certainly get invited back.

67 | is it worth investing in wine?

Wine has an advantage over other potential sorts of investment in that if the worst comes to the worst, you can always drink it. But it also has several disadvantages. It's bulky, it's fragile, it's sensitive to storage conditions, it deteriorates with time and it's not regulated in the way that stocks and shares are, with the upshot that there are numerous fake bottles in circulation.

Still interested in investing in wine? And here, I'm thinking of investment as making a financial gain over a period of time. If I haven't put you off, this is what you need to look for when picking a wine.

1) It has to be a great wine from a highly-regarded producer in a top-class vintage.
2) It has to be from a region in which there's a healthy secondary market – no point investing in something and then finding no-one wants to buy it.
3) You have to buy it as cheap as possible, which usually means the moment it's released. However...
4) You have to buy at a time when the market isn't overheated – in the past 10 years, many wines that fitted the above three rules have actually fallen in value.

In practice, this means that the wine investment market is mainly red Bordeaux, with smatterings of Burgundy, a few top Italians and Spaniards, and some high end Californian reds. They'll all be expensive – no point buying something only to find that any rise in prices has merely covered the storage costs – and you'll need to be prepared to hold onto them for several years.

Have I put you off? Hopefully I have. I want as many people as possible to drink good wine, and this sort of speculation only puts the world's top wines out of the reach of normal people.

68 | how long does wine last?

In the Speyer Museum in Germany, there's a bottle of what is presumed to be wine that dates back to the 4th century. It doesn't appear to have changed much since it was discovered in 1867, in part thanks to the large amount of olive oil that was originally added to preserve it, but if anyone does ever break its seal and sample it, chances are that it will be more "interesting" than tasty.

How long a wine remains in an attractive condition is largely dependent on its constitution. Four substances found in grapes help a wine age: acidity (think of pickling), tannin, as used in tanning leather, sugar (jam anyone?) and alcohol – remember those creepy specimen jars in the biology lab? If a wine has a framework of some of these in sufficient amounts, and a depth of flavour sufficient to fill in that framework (very important), it should in theory age well. Vintage Port for example has all four in abundance, and is one of the longest lived wines around.

(There's a fifth substance that has historically been important in keeping wines in good condition, namely sulphur. It's produced naturally as part of fermentation, but is also added at various stages throughout production to act as a preservative. Recent years have seen a reduction of use of sulphur in many cellars both in order to reduce chemical additions and to make the wines more attractive at an earlier stage. However, there are some who feel that this has reduced the wines' ageability, and we're now seeing some producers increasing their use of sulphur once again.)

But not all vintage ports are created equal. Some can happily be consumed before their 10th birthday, while others need more than twice as long to reach their peak, and then remain enjoyable for several decades more, before fading gently into a still interesting old age. And it's similar for all wine styles. Some New Zealand Sauvignon Blancs are absolutely ready at six months old, while others need a year (and sometimes two) in bottle to calm down.

69 | this one is older than that one – does that mean it's better?

Let's start by heading back fifty years, to a time when not a great deal was known about the science of wine production. The grapes arriving at many wineries tended to be less than perfectly ripe and were often unhealthy, while the winemaking veered towards the "industrial".

The result was young reds that were often coarse and tannic. Aging, both in barrels and subsequently in bottles, mellowed these brutes – eventually... It's said of some mid-19th century Bordeaux reds that they only became ready to drink after the original buyers had died.

As for the young whites, many were tart (from early picking) and dosed up with sulphur dioxide (SO_2) to both keep them fresh and stop refermentation of any sugar left in the wine. Unfortunately, the SO_2 also muted the wine's flavours, in some instances for several years.

Today's wines are softer, riper and cleaner, and don't need lengthy aging. In the majority of cases, DYA – Drink Youngest Available – applies, especially with whites and rosés. However, as you'll see in the next chapter, there are some wines that do benefit from keeping....

70 | how can you spot a wine that will age well?

As I mentioned above, most wines sold today, especially in supermarkets, fall into the DYA category. However, there are some that (in winespeak) have a long drinking window, in other words they're capable of giving pleasure over a number of years, and others where DYA means you miss out on drinking the wine at its best. These are the ones we're on the look-out for and you can identify them using what I call the Weekend Wine Test...

An early indication that a wine could be a keeper is that the last glass, drunk a couple of hours after the bottle was opened, is noticeably better than the first. So on a Friday night, open another bottle, pour yourself a glass, and taste it, ideally not at breakneck speed. Think about how fresh it is, how much you enjoy it, how much it changes in the glass as you swirl and sniff it. Then stick the cork back in and put the bottle away in a cool place.

(Yes, yes, I know the thought of opening a bottle of wine and not finishing it at one sitting is alien to many people, but this is scientific research we're doing here, so show some discipline...)

Repeat this on the Saturday and then the Sunday nights, thinking about how the wine has changed, and whether it has been for the better. If the freshness has faded leaving flavours that aren't that great, you'll know it's a DYA wine. But if your favourite is the Sunday glass, you have a candidate for keeping.

In which case, buy a few bottles, stash them somewhere appropriate (see the next chapter), and make a note to try the first one after six months. In the meantime, repeat the Weekend Wine Test with a different wine every few weeks, with the view of expanding your fledgling wine cellar. Or wine cupboard. Or wine suitcase-under-the-bed.

71 | how should I store my wine?

The ideal place to keep wine is cool, dampish and dark, and doesn't fluctuate much from month to month. Since large parts of northern England fit these criteria, maybe I should be a little more precise.

Cool: Leave milk out on a hot day, and it turns rancid. Keep it in the fridge and it stays fresh. Wine is the same. The cooler the conditions, the slower the wine will deteriorate. But don't let it get near freezing point.

Damp: While it's not too important for wines that have screwcaps, some humidity is beneficial for wines that have corks. If the air is too dry, the corks are at risk of drying out, which could compromise the seal. This is why bottles with corks are best stored on their sides rather than standing up (if it's humid and your bottle labels begin to perish, you can spray them with varnish to preserve them).

Dark: It's not just our skin that suffers if exposed to too much sunlight. Just as you can have corked wines, so too there are "light-struck" wines. An excess of light, both natural and artificial, results in wine losing some of its aromas and flavours, so keep your bottles in the dark, especially when they're made of clear glass.

Fluctuations/Vibrations: The more you have going on in your life, the faster you mature. Ditto for wines.

Some homes have cellars that fit the cool/damp/dark/ vibration-free criteria perfectly, but most don't. So you're going to have to simulate those conditions somehow. If you can afford a special wine fridge (Google them), then great. If not, look around for those corners of your house that can be adapted for use. An under-stair cupboard. A suitcase or two lined with bubble wrap under the bed. A corner of the garage that's not exposed to extremes of temperature. Or maybe you're just going to have to move to one of those parts of northern England...

I have a question about...

Serving Wine

72-81

72 | at what temperature should wine be served?

Simple. Not too hot, not too cold. Too hot, and the wine will lose its freshness. Too cold and not only will the flavours be muted, but any tannin in the wine will poke out like an unwanted pustule on prom night.

Giving a precise figure is a bit pointless. You pour a wine at 12°C in a room at 21°C and put it into the hand of someone whose body temperature is 37°C. What temperature will it be after ten minutes? Hmm...

Most white wines are served too cold. An hour or two in the fridge is OK, a day is too long (unless the wine is dreadful and you want to eradicate its personality). And many reds are served too warm because someone's heard they should be at "room temperature". Where's the room, Rome or Helsinki? And are we in the era of central heating and air-conditioning or of coal fires and woolly underwear? So don't be afraid to serve your reds straight from that cool corner where you store your wines – if they're a bit on the chilly side to start with, warm rooms and warm hands will soon change that.

73 | do I need different glasses for different wines?

"Need", no. Simple as. I'm probably not alone in having supped rather good wine from something as humble as a paper cup and enjoyed the experience. If however you're wondering whether your wine drinking pleasure will be enhanced by having a range of glasses, then that's a different matter.

To those in favour of having a large variety of glasses, I'd ask you to Google "Gourmet Magazine Shattered Myths". You should be able to find an article detailing how claims that wines can taste significantly different depending on the size and shape of the glass didn't prove exactly robust under scientific scrutiny.

However, wine wasn't meant to be drunk in experimental conditions in a laboratory. I've just done an impromptu survey of my wife and daughter to find out how they feel when they're wearing the "right" clothes. The general feel was of a boost in morale: the phrase that stuck out was, "You walk taller."

It's the same with wine glasses. Something served in an elegant crystal goblet is going to seem better to most people than if it were to come in a chipped tooth mug. So if having a beautiful array of different glasses on your table enhances this impression, by all means go for it. Just don't blame me when it's time to wash up…

74 | you haven't filled my glass up to the top - why not?

You have a bedroom, right? Is that absolutely full? No, didn't think so, otherwise you wouldn't be able to take off your clothes or turn over in bed at night. You have a car?

And do you always cram as many people into the back seat as possible? No, it would be a bit constricting, wouldn't it? And when you have a meal in a restaurant, do you complain if you can still see some of the plate? No, or at least not outside certain parts of northern England.

In the same way, wine is all the better for having room to spread out. Fill a glass to the brim and not only will your precious plonk be reluctant to reveal its lovely aromas, but you'll probably spill some when you pick it up. So if a sixth of a wine bottle (=125ml) comes much more than a third of the way up the glass, treat yourself to bigger glasses.

75 | those bits in my wine – what are they, are they harmful, and how do I deal with them?

First, bits of cork. Sometimes the cork crumbles when a bottle is opened, and bits of it end up in your glass. This doesn't mean the wine is "corked" (more of that in Chapter 60), just that you have a lump of cork in your wine, which can easily be fished out with a spoon.

It's more of a problem when the cork disintegrates, leaving a film of dust on the surface of the wine. It's usually only an issue with the first glass of wine – subsequent ones tend to be dust-free. To rescue that first glass, if you have a spare pair of (clean) tights to hand – and curiously not everyone does – strain the wine through them into a fresh glass. Otherwise do your best fishing with a spoon and be more careful with the bottle next time. If this happens in a restaurant, show the waiter what the problem is and let them deal with it. You may find they open a new bottle.

Second, some wines have diamond-like crystals in the bottom of the wine and on the surface of the cork. These are tartrates, and not only are they harmless, they also show that the wine underwent less manipulation prior to bottling. Sometimes wines go through a process called cold stabilisation in order to encourage the tartrates to precipitate out. While this makes for a clearer wine, it can also have an impact on the wine's flavour.

Finally, sediment. The flaky bits on the base and sides of a bottle form when substances such as colour compounds, yeast cells, tannins and tartrates link together, become too heavy to stay in suspension and fall to the bottom. As with tartrates, these could be taken as an indication of quality: filter them out too zealously and you risk losing some of the flavour too.

The older and darker the wine, the more sediment there'll be – mature vintage port has it in spades, and you can often see it in bottles if you hold them up to a bright light. It's harmless but unsightly, so you might want to decant the wine off it.

Three tips for decanting. Firstly, stand the bottle up, ideally at least a couple of days before you open it, to let most of the sludge gather on the base. Secondly when you open the bottle, pour it out into your jug/decanter in one long, smooth movement. Thirdly, as soon as you see wispy sediment passing through the neck of the bottle, stop pouring, or at least pour the rest into a separate wine glass. Which you can then drink, or use for your gravy.

But there's another reason to decant wine, which we'll look at in the next chapter...

76 | what is "breathing"? why should I decant wines?

I'm going to deal with these together, as they're closely related. We've just seen one reason for decanting wine, but sediment isn't the only reason to do it.

So on to the other reason. Have you ever had that experience of the first glass of wine from a bottle tasting noticeably different from the last? Some wines – like some people – hardly change in personality over time. Others however begin to reveal traits that you initially missed. Or maybe they behave like raw chicken. Sometimes when you unwrap uncooked chicken, it initially smells a bit iffy, only for the pong to blow off after a few minutes. Wines can be like that: people talk about "bottle stink". And finally there are those wines where the second glass is worse than the first – but better than the third...

In general, it's those two middle types of wines – those with hidden personality traits and those of the raw chicken variety – that benefit most from "breathing". More of how you identify them in a moment, first, a bit about what breathing is and is not. Opening a bottle and just leaving it there has little effect on the wine. That's not breathing, that's sitting there with your mouth open. In order to get the wine to open up and come out of its shell, you need to decant it. Which you know how to do now having read the previous chapter.

How long should that breathing time be? And how can you tell whether a wine needs it? The easiest way is open the bottle an hour or so before serving and have a sip. If it seems fine, then stick the top back on and forget about it till later. Most whites, especially cheaper ones, will be fine straight from the bottle, whereas many reds, and not just the expensive kind, benefit from a little aeration. So slosh the wine into your jug and give it a swirl around – if the jug's not very pretty, you can always pour the wine back into the bottle just before serving. Experiment, learn from your experiences, and tweak the breathing time accordingly.

77 | I've got a really old bottle of wine, should I decant it? and if so, how far in advance?

Old wines are like old people. Some of them are still in excellent condition, while others are fading rapidly. They can be in tip-top form one day only to clam up the next. Sometimes they need time to loosen up to be seen at their best, while at other times they're in fine fettle from the word go. In other words, you can't predict what they're going to be like in advance.

So proceed with caution. Here's what I do – it might not be the classic method but it works for me. Before I open the bottle, I stand it up for at least a couple of days in advance – a week is better. Then an hour before I'm going to drink it, I get four things ready: a wine glass, a decanter/jug, my corkscrew with the longest possible thread – old corks are fragile and crumble all too easily – and a 20cm saucepan. Yes, you read that correctly, a 20cm saucepan.

I gently open the bottle and immediately pour a small measure into the glass, but rather than returning the bottle to the vertical, I rest it at an angle in the pan, in order not to disturb the sediment at the bottom. Then I taste the wine. Does it feel like it's still strong and vigorous, and would benefit from the chance to open up further? If so, into the jug/decanter it goes for an hour (see the previous chapter). Does it seem absolutely ready to drink? If so, I'll leave it in the bottle, and then pour out measures later as required, each time being as careful as possible not to shake up that sediment.

And sometimes you'll have that first sip and it will be clear that the wine has had it. It could have been down to poor storage, it could have been a bad cork, or it could just be that the wine wasn't meant to last that long. It happens, but hopefully as you get more experienced with wine, it'll happen less and less.

78 | what's the best way to cool down wine quickly?

I've no problem with people using ice cubes for basic wines, providing they're aware that their wine's going to become diluted as the ice melts (if this is a concern, try using frozen grapes instead). But better wines deserve a little more TLC. My favourite way is with special cooling sleeves that can be kept in the freezer and then pressed into action when required. With these, a warmish bottle can be chilled in five minutes or less. If you don't have these, a pan filled with ice, water and a spoonful of salt works just as quickly, although you might lose the bottle label in the mixture. And if you're going to shove it in the freezer, wrap it in frozen peas or a wet tea towel and DON'T FORGET ABOUT IT. I'm sure I'm not the only one who's found cracked bottles and wine slushies the morning after...

79 | can I add things to my wine?

No. Haven't you seen those back-label stickers saying, "Anyone caught adding anything whatsoever to this wine will be fed only fish fingers for a year"?

There is of course nothing to stop you adding anything to a wine. In fact, while I'd keep the additives out of upper-tier bottles, many cheap wines are all the better for a bit of hacking. A chunk of ice to chill it down (and mute the flavours), some fruit juice and spirits to give flavour and oomph, herbs and/or spices à la mulled wine, some soda water to make it into a long drink, some lemonade for sweetness and fizz, and so on. Don't be afraid to experiment. But if I see you doing it with a bottle of something really decent, I'll sit on your prize Pomeranian.

80 | what's the best wine to serve at weddings?

When did weddings become so complicated? Shouldn't the idea be for two people to declare undying love to each other in the company of their friends and family, and for everyone then to have a party? I'm approaching this question in that spirit, which means following the general rules for party wine. So don't buy anything you wouldn't want to sup yourself, but don't overspend, as most people won't notice what they're drinking.

Many wedding venues force you to choose from their hugely overpriced banqueting list, so take this into consideration when you choose somewhere for your reception. If you can negotiate a BYO deal, whereby you bring your own wine and pay a corkage fee for each bottle opened, you'll probably be able to drink better and save money too.

If you want me to pick some actual wines, here goes...

Fizz: Decent Prosecco – it's half the price of so-so Champagne, isn't as sharp and goes far better with wedding cake.
White: Pinot Grigio is safe but a bit ho-hum. How about something fresh but intense like Spain's Verdejo (from Rueda) or Godello (from Valdeorras or Monterrei)?
Rosé: Chilean Cabernet is good in red form, but the rosés can also be rather tasty.
Red: Côtes du Rhône-Villages or Argentine Malbec. Sensible price, lots of flavour.

Yes, it's a very mainstream selection, but the idea is to having something tasty but not so fascinating that it draws attention away from the day's proceedings. Happy...?

81 | once it's open, within what length of time should a bottle of wine be drunk?

All wines are different. Some are tasty when they're opened, but then began to fade – as in lose their freshness and charm – within an hour. Others are dumb as a dodo initially, and only reveal their true colours with time – I've had bottles that were still improving three or four days after I first pulled the cork.

However, these latter ones are the exceptions. In general, most wines, will be at their best on Day 1. You can extend their lives by storing them in the fridge overnight (reds as well as whites), but while they certainly won't do you any harm if you keep them for longer than that, you will notice that they're looking more and more tired with each day.

There are several products designed to prolong the life of your wine, but the only affordable ones I'd recommend are ones such as Private Preserve and Winesave where you squirt some inert gas into the bottle to displace the air inside. And even with these, I'd hesitate to keep opened bottles much longer than a week.

A final word about sparkling wine. Given the chance, good fizz keeps its sparkle for a surprisingly long time – don't be surprised if there are still bubbles around after two or three days, even without using one of those purpose-made stoppers. If you want to put a silver spoon in the neck of the bottle to preserve the fizz, check out the range from www.overpriced-bling-for-gullible-people.com.

I have a question about...

Food and Wine

82-91

82 | what are the best food and wine combinations? and the worst?

Ready for this? I am not going to tell you. I could give you a few pointers as to the effect certain elements in food have on a wine's flavour, such as...

- Acidity in food reduces the perception of a wine's acidity.
- Fat in food decreases perception of a wine's tannin.
- Protein in food decreases perception of a wine's tannin.
- Salt in food decreases perception of a wine's acidity and tannin.
- Sugar in food increases the perception of a wine's acidity, and decreases perception of a wine's sweetness.

But when it comes to formulating rules of food and wine matching, the only one I'd advance is that if you combine people you like with food you like and wines you like, then you're 99% sure of having a good time.

We all have different sets of taste buds, and a combo that seems great to me might grate with someone else. For example, I find some mushroom dishes make certain wines, especially Pinot Noir, appear metallic, yet the Pinot/mushroom partnership is one that many people swear by. The fresh coriander that I love tastes like soap to some people. And those grippy tannins in red wines that many seek out just say "bitter and nasty" to others.

There's no such thing as a universal palate, and there's no such thing as a universal set of food & wine rules. Apart from that the food, the wine and the company should all, to quote Bill & Ted, Be Excellent...

83 | what is a "food wine"?

There are some wines where if you drink them on their own, the tannin or acidity (and often both) is of such a level that it pokes out to the point of distraction. This distraction level varies from person to person. Some people love their tea strong and tannic, others don't, and some like sour sweets such as acid drops while others hate them. But in general, a food wine is one that seems awkward by itself but blossoms in the company of appropriate food.

What you put in your mouth can have a startling influence on the flavour of what you put in straight afterwards. Toothpaste followed by orange juice is a classic example. When it comes to wine, there are certain elements in food that alter your perception of acidity and tannin both positively and negatively. If a wine's too tart, serve it with some food that's well salted, maybe with a bite of acidity (you could squeeze a lemon over it if you like), and it will seem much more rounded. And if chewy tannin is the issue, this should calm down if the food alongside is rich in fat and/or protein, and again isn't shy on the salt front.

(The converse of this is that some wines that taste good by themselves actually start to taste bland and lacking freshness when you have them with a meal, especially if they have a touch of sweetness.)

Most traditional wines from Europe developed alongside complementary cuisines, and it's often these that fall into the "food wine" bracket. Most often, you'll find a dark and tannic red wine that is tough going by itself but which comes into its own alongside a rich, fatty local meat dish. If you're ever in Portugal for example, try red Bairrada with leitão, the local name for suckling pig. Wonderful.

84 | in what order should wines be served at a meal?

The traditional progression is to start lighter and whiter and drier and then get heavier, redder and sweeter as the meal goes on. However, there are no wine police who are going to arrest you if you do it the other way round. I know producers who make beefy Shiraz which they drink as an aperitif. Some people like their sweet wines right at the start of a meal, others at the end. Don't bog yourself down with rules. If the move from one wine to another feels a bit clunky, just have a drink of water and a nibble on a piece of bread. And remember for next time...

85 | why is wine so expensive in restaurants?

Funny how it's usually wine that is singled out here, rather than other drinks. Consider Starbucks for a moment. Not a restaurant, but at least a place where cash is exchanged for drinks. Apparently the cup and the stirrer cost around twice as much as the coffee that went into that cup.

So is Starbucks ripping people off? Well, when you factor in utilities, training, shop rental, wages and other costs, not really. It's the same with restaurants and wine. The reasons that bottle of wine that costs £15 online has suddenly become £40 on the wine list is that glassware, service and storage of what is a bulky, fragile and sensitive product all have to be paid for.

If you are going to complain about mark-ups in restaurants, direct your zeal at bottled water and other soft drinks. And ask yourself how much the ingredients in that admittedly very tasty bowl of soup really cost...

86 | what are the best wines to order in a restaurant?

A question that raises more questions. What sort of restaurant are you in? What are you eating? Which wines do you enjoy? What's your budget? And there are probably more.

So I'm going to answer a different question, namely which are the best VALUE wines to order in a restaurant. No, it's not the Second Cheapest Wine (Google that for a video that hits the nail on the head). In fact, in most restaurants it's the wines at the cheap end of the list that have the highest percentage mark-ups.

Also, there are certain wines that people are always going to order regardless of quality – Pinot Grigio, New Zealand Sauvignon, Argentine Malbec, Sancerre and Chablis spring to mind. Is it any surprise that many restaurants try to find the cheapest possible and then slap on a hefty mark-up?

To find value, look for wines that are not mainstream, either in terms of region or grape variety. So if you like Argentine Malbec, try a red made from the less familiar Bonarda. If it has to be Sauvignon, how about one from South Africa rather than the Loire or New Zealand? And make use of the knowledge of the sommelier or waiter. In good restaurants, they'll know the gems on the list better than anyone, and will be more than happy to steer you towards them.

But do go to a restaurant prepared to pay a level above the cheapest bottles on the list. You don't use a similar policy when it comes to the food, and you shouldn't do it where wines are concerned either.

87 | I get embarrassed trying to pronounce all those foreign names – anything I can do?

Yes. Get over it. There are words and phrases and people that we all struggle with. Food enthusiasts have had to come to terms with gnocchi, paella and bouillabaisse. Sports fans have wrestled with Wojciech Szczesny, Giannis Antetokounmpo and Kim Clijsters. Film devotees have struggled (and won) when faced with Shia LaBeouf, Saoirse Ronan and Chiwetel Ejiofor. Tourists manage to emerge unfazed from encounters with Leicester Square, Yosemite and Llangollen. And elsewhere in the drinks world, spirits lovers have recovered from their initial forays into Islay whisky, Cognac and Daiquiris of various types.

So what's the point fretting over Cahors, Cuvée and Carignan? Just open your mouth and set off. If you come across someone who recoils in horror when you say Ryesling rather than Reece-ling, they're probably not the sort of person you want to know anyway. And if they're a waiter, just ask them how to pronounce "gratuity".

88 | should I buy wine by the glass in a restaurant?

Yes, yes, yes and yes.

Yes number one, it gives you and your dining companions the chance to try different wines with different dishes at different courses rather than stick to just one or two things throughout the meal.

Yes number two, it enables you to experiment with the weirder and wackier sectors of the wine world.

Yes number three, it means that you can try an expensive or exclusive wine without having to splash out on an entire bottle. Many restaurants now use a system called Coravin that enables them to serve fancy wines by the glass without removing the cork from the bottle, so the range on offer can be very enticing indeed.

And yes number four, it's the perfect option for when a bottle would be just too much.

Any no-no's? One thing you may need to be wary of is how long the wines have been opened before your glass is poured. Good restaurants should have a swift turnover of their by-the-glass wines, so this shouldn't be a problem. However, in seedier establishments, you might need to proceed with caution. But then you're maybe being a little optimistic in expecting your local greasy spoon to have decent wines in the first place...

89 | how should I taste a wine in a restaurant?

It's no different from tasting a wine at home: swirl, sniff, slurp. If everything's as it should be, then great, get the waiter/sommelier to pour you and your fellow diners a decent measure.

But what if it's not OK...? You'll find an entire section starting with Chapter 57 about the ways in which a wine can be faulty, most of which you can (with practice) detect by smelling them*. So why taste the wine? I do it to check the temperature. Really cold wines are very reluctant to release all their charms, including those charms which aren't so charming. Sometimes, those flaws only become noticeable once the wine has had a chance to warm up. Conversely, many restaurants serve their red wines way too warm. If you taste something and it's not far off the temperature of the soup, ask if they have any cooler bottles. If they don't, get them to put it in an ice bucket for five minutes or so before they fill up all the glasses.

However, what if when you taste the wine, you just don't like it? Two scenarios. If the waiter/sommelier specifically recommended it, then tell them and they should (hopefully) replace it with something different. But if you chose it yourself, and there's nothing wrong with the bottle, then tough. Kind restaurants may offer a replacement if you explain the situation, but otherwise just chalk it up to experience.

* For this, you have to smell the wine in the glass, not the cork – not all corked wines have a whiffy cork. So why do restaurants sometimes give you the cork to sniff? Because they don't know any better.

90 | why does the waiter keep filling up my glass?

Because it makes you drink faster, so you order a new bottle sooner, so the restaurant makes more money, and so they're seen to be doing something, otherwise their manager may think they're surplus to requirements. If you want them to stop, just tell them. And if they persist in doing it, ask for the proportion of the service charge that relates to the drinks to be taken off your bill...

91 | does it matter which wine I use to cook?

Slightly fudgy answer coming – it depends. The oft-trotted out line is that you should cook using the wine you're going to drink with the dish. However, if a wine costs £20+,

I for one am slightly reluctant to splash it into the skillet in large quantities.

The longer you cook something, the less the wine you use matters. After a dish has had a day of marinating and four hours in an oven, I defy anyone to tell whether the cooking wine was any good. However if you're splashing something in at the last minute, then it will have an impact on flavour. So if a wine has lots of tannin, or it's very oaky, or it's very aromatic – yes Sauvignon Blanc, I'm thinking of you – that character will come through in the dish, usually not in a positive way. In contrast, adding a splash of good Madeira/Marsala/Oloroso a minute or so before you turn off the heat can be a Very Good Thing, especially with soups and sauces for meats.

Another thing that happens with longer cooking is a reduction in alcohol content. Add wine at the last minute, even to boiling liquid, and much of the alcohol remains. Cook it for several hours and it's virtually all gone. But if there's sweetness in the wine, that *does* stay in the dish, so only use sweeter fare if you think it'll go well with the other flavours.

Did you want a rule of thumb? Cook with the cheapest wine that you'd drink. How's that?

I have a question about...

Wine and Health

92-95

92 | is wine good for your health?

93 | how many calories are there in a glass of wine?

94 | how many glasses of wine can I drink if I'm going to be driving?

95 | which are the best wines for avoiding headaches and hangovers?

92 | is wine good for your health?

One day, the newspaper carries a story that wine is good for you. The next, there's another item saying it's not. So which is true?

They both are. On the negative side, there's the sobering news that if you drink too much wine, you'll die. On the positive, there's are millions of people who can bear testimony to the fact that a healthy lifestyle is made even better by a daily glass or two of wine.

There's an old Russian proverb that says, "Drink a glass of wine after your soup and you steal a rouble from the doctor." In other words, little and often is the way to go. It's far better to drink two or three bottles of wine over the course of a week than the same amount in a binge session followed by six days of abstinence.

Treat wine as a food to be enjoyed rather than a drug either to be avoided or taken to cure your ailments. Fill up that glass and keep stealing those roubles.

93 | how many calories are there in a glass of wine?

There are two main elements of a wine that have calories, alcohol and sugar. Let's look at sugar first. Freshly pressed grape juice is full of the stuff – measure for measure, it has around 50% more than Coca-Cola! But then the yeast kicks off the fermentation and that sugar is gradually transformed to alcohol. However, even the most efficient yeast can't transform all the sugar to alcohol. It will get through most of it, but will then leave maybe 1-2 grams of unfermented or residual sugar per litre of wine – or in shorthand, 1-2g/l RS.

Then there are some wines where the producer will leave a little RS in the wine to round out the flavours. Many New Zealand Sauvignons for example have 5g/l of RS, and some popular branded wines come in at 10-25g/l RS. And finally there are purposely off-dry to very sweet wines, in which RS levels can rise as high as 900 g/l of RS – read more about them in Chapter 12.

But for the moment let's look at a dryish wine with 5g/l of RS. A gram of sugar has 4 calories, so a litre of wine has 20 calories that are due to the sugar, and a 750ml bottle has 15 calories (I've no idea how many glasses you get out of a bottle so I won't give a per glass figure).

Not much, you say. But let's have a look at the alcohol. And let's use the example of a wine at 13% ABV. That means that 13% of a litre of that wine – so 130ml – is alcohol. With 1ml of alcohol weighing roughly 0.8 grams, and with alcohol having 7 calories per gram, we end up with a litre of wine having 130 x 7 x 0.8 = 728 calories, which means that a bottle has around 540 calories.

As you'll see, in most everyday wines, the sweetness has far less of an effect on the calories than the alcohol level, regardless of whether the wine is still, sparkling, red, white or pink. Food for thought. Or perhaps drink for thought...

94 | how many glasses of wine can I drink if I'm going to be driving?

Hmm... That's a bit like asking how much over the speed limit I can drive before I'm going to get caught. There are too many variables at play here to give a simple answer. How big is the glass, how strong is the wine, how long before driving will you be drinking, what size and sex are you, what state is your liver in, what is your metabolism like, what else have you been drinking and eating?

Actually, strike that, there is a simple answer. Get a taxi, get a bus or train, have soft drinks (see Chapter 43), just don't be an idiot.

95 | which are the best wines for avoiding headaches and hangovers?

The most common cause of hangovers? Drinking too much. Alcohol disrupts sleep, can upset your tummy and is a diuretic. So if you wake up the morning after feeling tired, queasy and dehydrated, you only have yourself to blame – you should have drunk less, eaten more, stopped drinking earlier and gone on to drinking water.

However, there are compounds in certain wines that do cause headaches in some people. Foremost among these is NOT sulphites. Sulphites are found in all wines, and most winemakers add them to their wines to act as a preservative. The level of sulphites found in wine is small compared with other foods. Do you have a problem eating dried apricots? If not, don't blame the sulphites in wine for your headache.

So what is the culprit? It's usually red wine rather than white that gets the blame, which would seem to suggest that there's something in the grape skins that's behind the headaches. Could it be tannins? Some studies have shown that tannin causes the release of serotonin, which in high concentrations can give rise to migraine-like symptoms. Read more about tannin in Chapter 58.

If you suffer the same reaction to smoked fish, preserved meats and aged cheeses that you do to wine, histamines may be the cause. Those who take antihistamines for hay fever could try taking one before setting into the wine – and red wine in particular, where the histamine levels are significantly higher than in whites.

Or it could be prostaglandin. Or tyramine. Or biogenic amines. Or something else. The truth is that there doesn't seem to be one single cause of wine headaches. Maybe you should keep a note of the wines that seem to bring it on more than others. And of how many glasses of each brought it on...

I have a
question
about...

Practical
Wine Matters

96-101

96 | where do I go to learn more about wine?

Reading about wine in books and specialist magazines can be useful, but you need to combine the practical with the theoretical. There's no point swotting up on wine if you don't taste the stuff and compare notes with others.

The first port of call for this should be your local wine shop. Virtually all decent ones will have bottles open at the weekends (or at least they will in countries where this is permitted) and providing you don't abuse this hospitality, the staff will normally be very willing to share their knowledge and answer your questions.

The next stage is to go to some paid events. Most wine merchants hold large tastings once or twice a year where you have the chance to taste a far wider range of wines. Definitely worth the entry fee, especially as you often get it knocked off purchases on the night. Many will also have a fuller programme of dinners and tastings, often with winemakers in attendance, and some will even organise their own educational courses.

If your local merchant doesn't have these, check out whether the WSET (Wine & Spirit Education Trust) runs a course in your area. There are simple ones for beginners, leading up to the Diploma, which requires two years of study. More intense still is becoming a Master of Wine, the top qualification of the wine world. But even having the initials MW after your name doesn't mean you know everything about wine. There are always emerging regions to visit and new producers to discover. The good news is that this sort of learning is rather fun to do...

97 | what are the best wine regions to visit?

Are you talking about a day trip or a week? Is it going to be just wine, or do you want to do other activities – sport, culture, beaches – too? How important is the scenery? How into wine are your travelling companions? Are you a newbie or a nerd? Foot, bike or car? Are you prepared for people not to understand English?

While there's no one-size-fits-all wine region, here are five that do a decent job.

Alsace, France. Burgundy is wonderful, but I'm going to push the pleasures of Alsace instead, as it seldom receives the attention it deserves. There's great biking, skiing and walking nearby, castles, palaces and other historic buildings to visit, and a network of chocolate-box villages surrounded by vineyards and criss-crossed by the excellent Alsace Wine Route. And the food is delicious, and not quite as hearty and sausage-heavy as was once the case.

Chianti, Italy. Even without the excellent wine, this region between Florence and Siena would be worth a visit for the food, architecture and scenery. If you don't fancy driving, there's a bus from Florence that goes much of the way along the Chiantigiana, the road that cuts through many of the major wine villages such as Greve, Panzano and Radda. Avoid July and August if you can.

Franschhoek, South Africa. The French Corner is sometimes called the food and wine capital of South Africa, and also offers great shopping, whether you go for swanky boutiques or outdoor markets. If you're a walker, get yourself a permit to explore the Mont Rochelle Nature Reserve. For visiting vineyards, leave your car at home and either hop on the Wine Tram, which stops at various spots throughout the valley, or do a tasting tour on horseback.

Margaret River, Australia. It's becoming a bit gentrified, but there's still something of a cool beach vibe to Margaret River. Some wineries go big with visitor centres, restaurants and concerts in summer, others are still small family affairs, but the welcome everywhere is (usually) friendly. Away from wine, you can go surfing, whale-watching, bird-watching and riding, and there's also a network of caves to be explored.

Mendoza, Argentina. There are several wineries with tasting rooms in the City of Mendoza, but you're better served travelling out to places such as the Valle de Uco and Luján de Cuyo. And for non-winos, there's biking, mud baths, white-water rafting and Mount Aconcagua, the highest mountain in the southern hemisphere.

98 | what is the best way to travel with wine?

Being bulky, fragile and temperature-sensitive, wine is definitely not the easiest of travelling companions. So how can you make sure it arrives at its final destination in good condition? Some ideas...

1) Suits you. Those who fly regularly with wine might want to invest in a Vin Gard Valise, a special suitcase with a tough polycarbonate outer shell and durable foam innards that will take up to 12 bottles. Wine Check is an alternative

brand. But with both, make sure you weigh the packed case before you get to the airport otherwise the combination of heavy bottles and stingy luggage allowances might have you forking out some extra money.

2) Just in case. Many wineries and wine shops will pack wine in travel-ready containers that are meant to withstand rough treatment. Just be aware that some baggage handlers can take "rough" a little too far...

3) Pack it in. You can always take a chance and stash bottles in your luggage. In this case, the best way is to buy special cushioned bags for them. Some, JetBag for example, are reusable, others like WineSkin are not. Or simply wrap your largest jumpers and fluffiest towels around them and keep your fingers crossed.

4) Blowing hot and cold. If you're travelling by car on long trips, you need to take into consideration the outside temperature. If it's too cold, there's a chance the wine will freeze. If it's too warm, the bottles will be fine but the wine will suffer – which is why many wineries in California refuse to ship wines between June and September.

99 | I've inherited some wine – what's the best thing to do with it?

The choices are simple: drink it or sell it. If you take the first course, you don't need my advice – just pull the corks, toast the person who bequeathed you the wine and enjoy.

If you want to sell, maybe it's an idea to think of the wine like a car. Regarding its value, you need to ask two questions. Firstly, is the car/wine desirable? Even in mint condition, a 1970s Austin Allegro isn't going to have the buyers beating down your door, but a Triumph Stag of the same era might. In wine terms, you'll have far more customers for a dozen top end 2005 Bordeaux reds than for a stash of similarly venerable Aussie Chardonnays.

Secondly, can you provide FSH – full service/sellaring history? (bit of licence with the spelling there...) A car/case of wine that has had one careful owner from new will be worth considerably more than one that has a colourful but dubious past.

As for where to sell it, again the car analogy works well. You can do a private sale, go to a dealer for either a cash sale or a part-ex or put it into auction. Which course is best? That will depend on what you're selling, and whether you want your money sooner or later. It shouldn't take much research (wine-searcher.com is a good port of call) to get a rough idea of how saleable the wine is. If it's in demand, great. If it's not, then, hey, you didn't pay for it, why not crack open some of the bottles and see what they're like? You might be pleasantly surprised...

100 | how do you prevent wine staining your teeth?

I'm presuming you don't want me to say "only drink whites"... Those who taste wine professionally will be fully aware of just how Dracula-like their mouths can look after a lengthy session at the spittoon. While this means that you never have a problem getting a seat on public transport – one grimace, and the commuters flee – it isn't exactly the most endearing of appearances. And it's not just the pros who suffer: a couple of glasses of deeply coloured wine can transform your pearly whites into something rather murkier.

There's not much you can do to prevent this, but there are steps you can take to reduce the effect. You could try sticking to lighter-coloured reds such as Pinot Noir and Nebbiolo rather than Cabernet Sauvignon, Malbec and Shiraz, but that would restrict your choices, so I wouldn't recommend that. Instead, have one glass of water for every glass of red wine, and make sure you intersperse your drinking with some eating.

Whatever you do, don't be tempted either to brush your teeth or use the hand towels in the toilets to rub away the stains. Such steps may restore some of the whiteness, but they'll also strip the enamel from your teeth. If you must do something, chew some gum. It's slower on the stains than brushing, but it'll freshen your breath and is much kinder to your teeth in the long term.

101 | how do you get wine stains out of a carpet or shirt?

"Whoops…" It's happened to most of us. Maybe we chinked our glasses too vigorously. Maybe our aim was poor. Maybe we should have known the table was uneven, and the bottle was bound to tip over. But the result in each case was the same – a once-pristine carpet, jacket or skirt now with a large and growing red wine stain…

There are a number of theories on how to cope with such a situation. Some people advocate sprinkling the stain with salt. And it's true that salt will absorb some of the wine, but it won't get it all. Others say you should pour WHITE wine on to "neutralise" the stain. Hmm, not sure of the science here, but what about the effect? Well, the clearer liquid certainly succeeds in reducing the intensity of the stain. However, it also succeeds in spreading it over a larger surface area, not to mention making the smell of wine twice as strong.

There are better methods. Off-the-shelf stain removers such as Vanish work reasonably well, and there are some specially-made products such as Wine Away that are also very effective. If you don't have such things to hand, don't worry. Apply plenty of cold water to the stain, then dab (rather than rub) with a towel. Repeat both steps several times, and you'll soon have your clothes/carpet back in a reasonable if slightly soggy condition. Whichever method you choose, speed is of the essence – the longer you wait, the less likely it will be that you'll get rid of the stain.

In the future, this may no longer be a problem. The manufacturers of Labfresh shirts (and ties and socks) claim that their products are not only stain resistant but also odour resistant, wrinkle resistant and machine washable too. "A Labfresh shirt can be worn for many days in a row, and you still don't have to wonder if your date can smell how long a day you had." If they could now turn their hand to carpets, curtains and school uniform, the world would be a much better place…

www.simonwoods.com

@woodswine

"I Don't Know Much About Wine...
...But I Know What I Like"

After hearing that line for the 53rd time, Simon Woods decided it was time to address the problem. Hence this book, an easily digestible and irreverent guide to the fascinating but often confusing world of wine. It's a book aimed at all those millions of people who regularly crack open a bottle, and are beginning to ask, "What's next?"

The first edition won the prestigious Prix du Champagne Lanson Award for the **Best Wine Book Of The Year**. This revised second edition features chapters on apps and wine bars, and more besides, as well as new illustrations from Manchester illustrator Steph Coathupe.

Available at simonwoods.com and Amazon.